Daniel Bubar

His for Hungary

A narrative about the Life of Daniel Bubar

Nakhati Jon with Lydia Newman

Nakhati Media

@2025 by Nakhti Jon
Nakhati Media
All rights reserved

ISBN: 979-8-9857602-3-1

Kindle Direct Publishing

Unless otherwise noted, all Scripture quotes are from The Authorized (King James) Version.

For further comments and inquiries, please see Nakhati Jon on social media or my blog – nakhatijon.com

With special thanks to the Bubar family, we fondly remember Daniel and his parents, Paul and Shirley Bubar. Each of them completed the race that the Lord Jesus called them to. Although they have gone before us to their heavenly home, their memory will always bring a smile, knowing they followed the Lord joyfully and creatively.

To my daughter, Lydia: As a father, writing with you has been a pleasant jog down memory lane. I will always fondly remember our Panera outings as we attempted to work out the details of the narrative. I am thankful for the voice of narrative you brought to the book to give life to the events. Thanks for making this project such a joy.

To my wife: I sincerely appreciate you, who spent so much time on the text to help with my grammar issues and clarify my rambling. You have spent so much energy on this project, historically and presently, with your helpful insights. Thanks for walking with us in this endeavor; your touch on the book will improve the reader's enjoyment.

I am also thankful for the many who put effort into reading and editing the manuscript. Peggy Fleming was among the first readers to give some good early insights. Nancy Swanson, thanks for your willingness to pick up this project at the last moment to provide some needed edits. Also, for the final reader, Dee Parker, your attention to detail has continually improved my books.

Also, I am thankful to each of you who provided stories and experiences about Dan Bubar. Each encounter shared brought a fuller picture and a smile.

Foreword

"A bundle of stress poured out on people." That's how Dan's best friend, Jeff, described him. When Dan told us about that description, we laughed as a family. Truer words about my brother had rarely been spoken, but Dan was so much more than stress. He was perhaps one of the most determined, mentally tough and disciplined persons I have ever known. His eighth-grade teacher, Chuck Patterson, instilled in him a desire to become a runner. Dan was too short and too clumsy to ever become a great runner, so I thought. When Dan locked in on something, it was only a matter of time before it was going to happen.

With an iron will that had sorely challenged our parents in his childhood, Dan attacked running. Each year, he improved. His sophomore year, he placed in the top 20 in the annual Turkey Trot race. His junior year, he placed in the top five. His senior year, he was waking up at 5:00 a.m. to train. He was not going to be denied. The day of the race came, and the gun sounded. "Some guy shot out ahead of me and I lost sight of him," he later told me. Dan panicked. He picked up his pace but still no sight of the mystery speeding spoiler. Dan finally hit a part of the course that nobody had run on yet. It had snowed the night before and there were no footprints before him. "The guy must have taken off too fast and peeled off to puke somewhere and I missed him," he chuckled. I'll never forget the moment I saw him sprinting toward that finish line. I was so proud of him. He finished over a minute ahead of the next runner.

In the summer of 1993, I flew to Hungary and met up with Dan. He took me on a week vacation in the Czech Republic, where I would later serve as a missionary with Word of Life. We were exploring the possibilities of ministry in this country. There we were, just the two of us, neither spoke Czech, fumbling around and exploring Prague and the surrounding areas. We went to see an old castle and ended up meeting the owner, Duke Giovanni Kinsky. When he learned we were Americans, he invited us to stay for lunch. Dan was beside himself with excitement. About a year later, I began raising support to return to Czech, in large part because of that visit with my brother. Last summer, that ministry celebrated their 25th anniversary.

I'll never forget the night the phone rang and it was Eric Murphy, Dan's boss, asking to speak with my dad. Dad had gone to speak at a youth conference in Canada. I gave him the contact number of Dad's hotel and thought nothing of it. When he called back ten minutes later and asked for my mom, I became suspicious. Mom was at church. Five minutes later, Joe Jordan, the Director of Word of Life, called for my dad. "What's going on, Joe?" I asked. "Is something wrong with Dan?" Joe couldn't answer. He didn't want to break that news to me over the phone. Shortly after, there was a knock at the door. Some elders from our church were there to tell us that Dan had been in a bad accident, and it didn't look good. A week later, Dan crossed a greater finish line than the Turkey Trot. He crossed the finish line of his life. When I think of Dan, I think of the last words of the Apostle Paul in 2 Timothy 4:7-8, "I have fought the good fight. I have finished the course [race]. I have kept the faith. Finally, there is laid up for me the crown of righteousness which the Lord, the righteous Judge, will give to me on that Day, and not to me only, but also to all who have loved His appearing."

Dan attacked life. He attacked running. He attacked scripture memory and Bible quizzing. He attacked his calling. He attacked the Hungarian language. He approached life with a relentless intensity. His light burned briefly, but oh so brightly. I hope that you get a sense of this remarkable guy as you read this book. It is an intimate glimpse into the value of youth ministry, the necessity of biblical community and friendship, the struggle of calling and the legacy of faithfulness. May you be encouraged, may you be inspired, and may you be challenged by the testimonies of Jeff and Dan.

Jonathan Bubar

Introduction

After 30 years, I still miss my buddy, Daniel Bubar. Our lives intertwined at an early age, and we shared many key moments. We were both called to missions, and the ministry of Word of Life shaped our calls.

My memories of Dan Bubar follow me as I journey in ministry. His companionship, fun, and excitement for life bid me on to finish the race well—not to quit, not to stop, and surely not to stumble.

The researcher Stacey Dubois said, "Memory is not an impartial recording device." Her assessment is spot on. My memory in this writing is far from impartial. Yet, it serves and prompts me to record my impressions on how God worked, led, and protected Dan and me.

Dan and I met as young teenagers in the Word of Life Inn kitchen. From the point of acquaintance, I knew this kid was different. He took his call to the ministry seriously, even as a teenager. His diligence and commitment made his life worth emulating. We met as summer kitchen staff in 1981. Over the years, as I have traveled through Central Asia and the Middle East and passed once again through Pottersville, NY, I am reminded of the many adventures Dan and I enjoyed.

Calling takes on many different bents in today's world. During the 1980s and '90s, it seemed more straightforward. We both sensed God wanted us to do a particular thing, and this sense was our calling. This sense of God in our lives framed how we studied, worked, dated, and saved or spent our money. Somehow, we knew that faithfulness is measured in both the little and the significant areas of life, so in these things, we moved forward. We were not perfect teens, nor did we assume that our ministry was one that others should emulate, but we both loved Jesus.

In the Bible, David had Jonathan during his early developmental years. Jonathan was by his side during some very lonely times, and he strengthened David to become what God called him to do and be. When everyone seemed to distrust David, Jonathan resisted the social pressure and stood by his friend, allowing him to obtain politically what was rightfully Jonathan's. Both looked beyond the circumstances to see a plan from God that exceeded expectations, somehow knowing their time would be brief but consequential.

For most of us, the past is a mixture of fond memories and glimpses of trauma. While I had my fair share of traumatic events with parental breakup and the death of a few friends, when I reflect on my days with Dan, they all seem to fall into the background. We were fiercely passionate about the same things. Not everyone is blessed with a friendship bond akin to David and Jonathan's. It's hard to find a friend who understands you so well that your boyish talk becomes understandable to the other. But that's what Dan and I had.

Ironically, Dan's brothers are named David and Jonathan, but Dan paved the way for me to pursue God, just like Jonathan did for David. Even when he was younger, Dan was wise and courageous like Jonathan. And like Jonathan, it felt like his life was cut short too soon, yet we know that God's plan is good and that his timing is perfect. No one lives a day past God's will and dies a day earlier than appointed by God.

This story is about how Dan Bubar lived his calling and how his influence affected mine.

Chapter One - Life before Bubar

Everyone had things they were obsessed with as kids, and each phase seems to bring new obsessions.

When I was 12, I was obsessed with Abbott and Costello, which happened to air Sunday mornings on two of our three channels. Is it so wrong to devote one's Sunday to laughter? Laughter is a good thing. I never received any pushback on this decision until my friend, Tim Leonard, invited me to attend church with him on Sunday.

Initially, I told him I would come, but on Sunday, when Tim came to my door, I decided that "Abbott and Costello" sounded much more satisfying than heading off to church.

"Sorry Tim, I just woke up." I thought, *Liar!* "So, I must skip this time." *Double liar! C'mon, Jeff!* Tim was gracious and understanding, and he could tell I was bluffing my way out of going. I scurried to the TV when he shut the door and let the laughter commence. I wasn't feeling much guilt or remorse over skipping church or lying about it. However, I then realized that the two channels that played "Abbott and Costello" were airing the same movie that the other channel had shown the previous week or so. As I watched in disappointment, I bore through the comedy that I had just seen the week before. It was a very inconvenient morning. In this small way, God got my attention and had a good laugh Himself that Sunday.

Tim returned to my door the following Sunday to pick me up for church. I figured "Abbott and Costello" wasn't the most reliable source of satisfaction, so I might as well go to church. Maybe church would bring some good laughs. So, I followed Tim into the snowy driveway and onto the church bus.

In reality, it was just a school bus, so it didn't hold any fond memories for me. As a twelve-year-old, I was already riding the bus five days a week, and it was potentially the worst part of the day. I just wanted a break from all things school!

I entered the church, sulky from the bus ride. There were so many people, all strangers except for Tim, and I was (and am) an introvert. I caught a glimpse of the auditorium and saw rows and rows of pews, each seemingly more intimidating than the next, as they got nearer the stage. I sheepishly followed Tim toward a seat on the balcony, thankful we sat towards the back and blended in. I stayed quiet during the sermon, but when it ended, a song started.

Everyone stood up almost in unison, and sing-song voices and melodies flooded the room. I felt awkward and shy trying to sing, so I listened to the lyrics as they floated past my ears.

> *"Just as I am, without one plea,*
> *But that Thy blood was shed for me,*
> *And that Thou bidst me come to Thee,*
> *O Lamb of God, I come, I come…"*

As the "I come, I come" slowly resonated around the room, I thought, *Is that why I am at church today? Did God bid me to come? And did he really shed his blood for me, just as I am? Even though I lied about skipping church and wanted to watch my show more?*

> *"Just as I am, and waiting not*
> *To rid my soul of one dark blot,*
> *To Thee whose blood can cleanse each spot,*
> *O Lamb of God, I come, I come.*
>
> *Just as I am, though tossed about*
> *With many a conflict, many a doubt,*
> *Fightings and fears within, without,*
> *O Lamb of God, I come, I come."*[1]

The song kept emphasizing that you come to God just as you are. I had thought people close to God must be perfect, but I guessed they weren't. I had many fears and conflicts, and maybe I could come to God even with them. I was thinking about all these things and my life in general, and then Tim turned to me, asking, "Do you know for sure that you will go to heaven if you die?"

How is anyone supposed to answer that? "I hope so," I whispered back.

"But would you like *to know for sure*? Would you like to know Jesus, the one the song is about?" I nodded in response and followed him out of the balcony and down the stairs. We passed through a door where more pews centered the aisles. The next thing I knew, he was walking toward the front of the church. I could either stand alone in the aisle like a deer in the headlights or walk behind Tim and at least join him despite my embarrassment.

As everyone watched the few of us walking to the front, my mind raced. Was I going to be exposed for the sinner that I was? I wanted to disappear, but I took another step forward despite my fear. To my relief, once I reached the front, some people led us to a small room out of sight of the entire church.

I sat with Tim and Mr. Gibby Gruet[2], who showed me what I later learned to be the Romans Road.[3] As he explained these verses, I knew I had heard some of them before. When I attended a Baptist camp near Broome Center, NY, the counselors there explained similar things, but this time, I realized I needed Jesus to have my sins forgiven.

I recall the emphasis of Romans 5:8, that God loved me despite my sin. Then, the verses in Romans 10 stated that I needed to confess that Jesus is Lord and my Savior from my sins, who was raised from the dead, the counselor Mr. Gruet explained. To confess before God meant I needed to pray to him. At camp, I remember going forward for something but do not remember praying. Now, below the pulpit, what was then called the choir room, was where I prayed, confessing my sins and stating that Jesus is my Lord and Savior. I felt at peace as I sat there with Tim and Mr. Gruet. I felt thankful even though I didn't fully understand the importance of the decision I had just made. I trusted Jesus as my Lord, but on that day, I had no idea what that would mean for the rest of my life.

New Life – New Routines

After leaving church, Tim and I hopped back on the bus. The warmth bubbled within me as I thought about the life change I had just gone through. As I stared out the window at the pure white snow, the song from church kept echoing in my head about getting rid of the dark spot of sin. Despite the frigid cold outside, I knew I would be in church again the following Sunday.

Life was never the same after that day. My lifestyle started to change in ways that I hadn't expected. I *willingly* hopped on a school bus each Sunday to go to church. After a week, my sister, Janet, joined me, and then, a bit later, my younger brother, Jason, joined. The changes came slowly, but my new Sunday routine initially helped me change how I spoke about the Lord, refraining from using His name in vain. In our family, at least with my siblings, I responded with greater understanding and patience.

Every Sunday, the ministry buses would bring in new kids who were in the same shoes as I once was, and each bus had around three Word of Life Bible Institute (WOLBI) students on board. Since

Tim had many friends, he invited them all, and I met others on the bus. My constant friends were the WOLBI students who participated in the weekend ministry there. They sought to influence the bus kids spiritually and encourage us in Christ. These WOLBI students exemplified Christ and were so welcoming to me. I would spend time talking and joking with them. They encouraged me in my walk with Christ, so I quickly befriended them.

The church was called Perth Bible Church, but many people in this circle thought of it as a Word of Life (WOL) church because of the number of people affiliated with Word of Life there. The pastor of Perth at that time was Dr. Charles F. Scheide. He preached on Sundays and taught theology at the Word of Life Bible Institute (WOLBI) throughout the week, where he taught for over 40 years.[4] A bus of 30 to 35 WOLBI students came down each weekend to help with weekend ministries. On Saturday, the church had breakfast for those who worked on the Sunday bus routes. After this time, the WOLBI students (Word of Lifers or BI students) would arrive and be ready for Saturday's bus visitation to see who would come on Sunday. The WOL'ers would visit and get to know the riders and their home environment. On Saturdays, the bus captain and students shared the gospel or encouraged new contacts to come on Sunday.

I loved spending time with the WOL'ers. Everything about WOL filled me with enthusiasm and awe. Their friendships demonstrated that they valued and accepted me. As a middle school student, good friendships were a rare commodity, so I attached myself to their weekend circle as much as possible. I felt less enthusiastic whenever the students didn't come down for the weekend. The Lord used this teen desire to mature my faith, and I later realized that He used this fellowship to grow me in the faith and to pursue more time at Word of Life.

Dan's Word of Life Family

Meanwhile, for some, Word of Life was not a discovery. Dan Bubar's father, Paul, founded WOL Bible Clubs. So, for Dan, Word of Life was his life. He acknowledged Christ as his Lord at a young age because his parents shared the gospel with him. Kids like him already had twenty or so verses memorized and had probably committed to a quiet time every morning.

But despite that significant difference, we were raised in similar ways. We both grew up in small villages in New York. Both our fathers valued hard work and responsibility, and incidentally, they both felt that chopping and gathering wood was an effective way to instill a strong work ethic. Burning wood avoided the high costs of heating during New York's cold winters, appealing to frugal families like Dan's and mine.

In the Bubar family, their father would joyfully shout, "Boys, we are going to work today!" His excitement was infectious, making the experience one filled with positive memories. Dan was probably skipping down the hall and energized by the first glimpse of the sun's rays. The three brothers

Bubar Family - David (left) and Daniel (right), baby Jonathan - 1970

would then follow their father in doing the work, bantering back and forth the whole time, as boys do.

My dad didn't introduce the event with nearly as much excitement. On a day when school was canceled, I recall him passively calling out, "Grump, get up! We are going over to Grandpa's to chop wood." I forced myself out of bed and walked out of my room as if five pounds of iron had suddenly encased each foot. My stomping induced yet more comments on me being grumpy. My father probably didn't realize that the name Grump made me even crankier. After all, I was a middle-school-aged boy up at the crack of dawn!

Don Lough Jr., a soon-to-be mutual friend then and the future director of WOL, said, "If you know Dan the way I knew [him], you know that he loved people. He loved the souls of people. He was concerned and had a deep compassion for the lost. Even as a little boy, I remember sitting in his room when he was about twelve or thirteen. He would share with me about those he was talking to about his faith. Those he was discipling. Always excited and consumed with telling people about the good news of Jesus Christ."

Don and Dan attended Glens Falls Christian Academy before Mountainside Christian Academy in Schroon Lake existed. In chapel, they sang "Dare to be a Daniel." Don said, "I remember whenever we got to Dan's name in the song when he and I were sitting together, and we would yell out his name, *Dare to be a DANIEL* — we kind of cheered him on…" Dan, even as a young boy, had courage.

I did not know Dan during these early years, since we grew up about 90 miles apart. Allow me to explain some of my background, which will lead me to meet up with Dan in 1981.

Word of Life Club

In the summer of 1980, my church had another ministry called Word of Life Clubs for teenagers. Tim brought in about 20 kids from the Fonda area in New York, and the church did extensive outreach to families from my school area at the time. As a result, the church decided to establish a WOL youth club to reach young people from my school area. This club focused on reaching the youth in my public school. I did not know it then, but Dan's dad had started this WOL program, and indirectly, we connected through it.

I love structure and lists, and this program exuded doable actions, including daily quiet time, memorizing verses, attending club meetings, and completing Christian service assignments. Excited by the opportunity, I jumped in and got involved. The club was led by two young couples, Ron and Jill Green and Mark and Connie Lou Sebast, who did an excellent job connecting with the teens. Many of my friends in this club learned about Christ and experienced spiritual growth.

One day, Mr. Sebast told me that, as part of the program, I needed to read a book. "Ah, not a book!" I protested." You see, I'd had trouble reading in 1st and 2nd grade and hadn't liked books ever since. So, when he suggested I read the autobiography *Daktar: A Diplomat in Bangladesh,* I was filled with fear. I am unsure how it happened, but somehow, he persuaded me, and I brought the book home. Reluctantly, I started reading… and kept going! The book took me to a new place I knew nothing about. The author wrote about people and places I wanted to go and see for myself. This man had given his life and profession to the Lord, to make a difference in a Muslim land. I loved seeing God's call on his life and how God used him to bless others. I started to love reading.

So, *Daktar* was the first book I'd ever finished, and significantly, I started to love reading. The WOL Club program opened my eyes to the joy of reading and sparked a thirst for understanding how God guides each of us. I wanted another book like it.

After a year in the Club program and two years of BI students on my bus, I desired to learn more about the Bible and how to serve. Tim, my former classmate who invited me to church, now attended Perth Bible Christian Academy. He as a role model encouraged me to desire to learn more and I wanted to go there as my next step in learning.

Chapter Two - Word of Life Inn - 1981

Soon afterwards, I approached Bob Calhoun, the associate pastor at our church.

"Are there any job openings at the church or in the area?" I asked. "Because if I could find summer work, then I could earn money to attend the Christian School in the fall."

He said, "That's interesting you asked. I just got off the phone with Don Lough (Senior) at the WOL Inn, and they are looking for summer staff."

Wow, really? I hadn't imagined this as the next step, but I applied to Word of Life Inn, sensing the Lord's leading.

My pastor said Mr. Lough was looking for teens to work in "the dish pit," so I checked this job first, hoping to increase my chances. Eventually, three of us from Perth ended up in the dish pit at WOL Inn for the summer, and I wondered what kind of new venture God had in store for me. In fact, it was the beginning of a journey that would increasingly draw me toward WOL and Dan.

Arrival at WOL Inn

I lied in bed that morning unable to sleep because I was so excited about heading to camp for the summer, I hoped to find some new friends in this kitchen camp atmosphere. The summer before, I worked briefly at a camp, and in that setting, work was more fun than hard.

With this anticipation, in mid-June 1981, my dad drove me to the Word of Life Inn — a place I heard about at snow camp but had never seen. I signed up to spend my whole summer working there. Maybe another kid would say working was no way to spend the summer, but as we drove up those roads and saw all the beautiful trees and the glistening Schroon Lake, I knew this was the perfect place to spend my summer. The entire area felt laid-back and peaceful. I was optimistic that I would form new friendships and experience personal growth amid all the work, learning to serve God from the heart.

Word of Life purchased the Inn property in 1953 as a conference center. Previously, it was known as the Brown Swan Club, with an

Adirondack flair. WOL ran this property as a spiritual resort with the foremost Bible teachers until 2019.[5]

Once we arrived, my dad parked, and I quickly hopped out of the car, stretching after the two-hour car ride. I saw a small building with a sign reading, "STC Office."[6]

I knew this was where I would check in — the Summer Training Corps (STC). After entering, we handed in the final necessary papers. A man at the entrance greeted me happily.

"Hey, welcome!" the man called out. "I'm assuming you're part of our summer staff?" I nodded and gave him my name. As he looked through his list, I decided to keep the conversation going. "The grounds are so nice, and I'm so excited to be staying here for the whole summer." He nodded in agreement but then started chuckling.

"Well, according to this list, you won't stay on these grounds." My face fell slightly, enough for him to notice, but he quickly said, "Don't worry, you'll be just down the road, not more than 500 feet or so." I tried to maintain my excitement.

The dorm was one of two buildings near the Island dock parking. On the plus side, it was conveniently located right by the water, as the parking was reserved for guests who took the boat to the island.

Once I got all my things situated, my dad drove me back to the Inn so I could get lunch. Just before entering the dining room, a man called my name. I was shocked because he didn't look familiar, but I walked over to him.

"Hello, how do you know my name?"

"I have been praying for you and recognize you from your picture. My name is Don Lough. We at the Inn are grateful for your willingness to serve with us this summer."

"Thanks, I'm excited to be here." I nervously ran my hand through my hair, knowing it was too long according to the Word of Life standards they'd sent me. "And I'll be completely ready to work once I get my hair cut. I'm planning to get it cut as soon as possible," I added, hoping he wouldn't see me as a rebel.

"Well, whenever that may be, and I'm glad you're here. I hope you enjoy your summer." He smiled at me. At that point, my dad knew I was in good hands and, after a quick goodbye, headed back.

As I sat among a room of other teens that I was soon to get to know, I felt ready for the adventures the summer had to offer. My father was gone, and I was away from home. It felt like a whole new world welcoming me in.

Meanwhile, Dan was packing his bags for a four-week discipleship adventure on the Island. This discipleship program took a group of young teens through outdoor camping experiences accompanied by in-depth Bible study. The program was designed to develop leaders among these teens.

The Pit

On Monday, after breakfast, the dish pit crew gathered for orientation. Sporting my Donald Duck t-shirt and a fresh haircut, I was ready for the kitchen work.

My supervisor led me to a black mat before an enormous double sink. He quickly showed me the washing sink, rinsing area, and flat area for drying. After he left, I stared up at the pile of pots and pans from breakfast. This was clearly more than what I was used to doing at home. "It's just dishes," I told myself as I grabbed the first pot.

Ten days passed, and I was still stepping on my tiny black mat every day to scrub pots and pans. As a 14-year-old with no seniority, this became my station. All the others preferred to work at the dish machine, so I didn't ask to learn how to use it. I didn't want to take away the preferences of others, and by that point, I was comfortable on my little black mat with my scraper sponge. I felt like I met more of the kitchen staff because everyone came to me to bring their pans that needed special cleaning.

One day, I hastened to finish up the last couple of dishes so that I could leave early. I glanced over at the pit crew by the dish machine. They were all laughing and joking together, as they were at the end of their workday. One grabbed the water hose and sprayed another kid with it, which summoned only more laughter.

"Hey, sorry I didn't bring these earlier. I accidentally burnt a bunch of gunk on the bottom of these pans." I looked over as someone from the kitchen piled two metal trays on top of the other pots I was trying to finish. I stared at the looming pile of kitchenware in agony. I was secluded and trapped on my tiny black square, with more work to do, while the other guys were laughing and enjoying their time on the dish machine. As I took on this challenge, other pans and sheets started appearing from various points in the kitchen.

My jealousy bubbled within me, and my thoughts became bitter and bitingly sarcastic. I tried changing them. *Looks like those dishes are too hot anyway*, I reasoned in my head. *They probably burn their hands all the time because of the dish machine. Who wants to work over there, anyhow? Boy, I love scraping burnt milk off the bottom of this pot! I love washing pots and pans!*

With every thought, I scrubbed harder, taking my frustration out on the dishes. Finally, I finished all the dishes in front of me. I looked over at the vacant dish machine. I hadn't noticed how quiet it had gotten since the rest of the dish pit had already finished their job. I flung off my water-soaked apron and waved a quick goodbye to the head chef. I returned to my room, slumped on the bed and quickly grabbed my journal. *"June 22, 1981 - Today was really hard work. I am about to die."*

While I was struggling with my job at the Inn, Dan was enjoying his program on the Island. Only a bit of water separated us, and a few weeks of time—we would be in the same kitchen.

After another couple of days of struggling on the secluded black mat, my supervisor, Mike, took pity on me.

"It seems like you've been doing the pots and pans this whole time, right?"

"Yeah, my daily task, which no one else wants, and I don't know how to work the dish machine." I gave him a half smile to try to be a good sport.

"Well, you can't do the pots and pans forever. I'm sure your hands are sore from all the scrubbing." I nodded at him, thinking about the aching joints in my hand. "We'll get you learning the dish machine right away," he encouraged me.

"Oh, the pots aren't that bad. I'm okay, really—" I fumbled over my words.

"Here," he guided me to the actual dish pit and handed me a hot dish. "Just grab these hot dishes that come through the machine, stack them, and put them in their designated spots. They come out hot, so they dry quickly." The dishes were steaming hot in my hands, but I welcomed it compared to the scrubbing I had endured for days. Mike stayed by my side for a while, showing me where dishes and glasses were placed. I learned quickly because of him; eventually, I was on my own.

I looked at the poor guy who had to take the despised place on the black mat. The pots and pans truly tested one's strength to do all to the glory of God. Before any good friends came along, the Lord wanted to nudge my heart attitude. During that summer, at one of the staff devotions, one of the speakers mentioned Colossians

14

3:23, *"Whatever you do, work heartily, as for the Lord and not for men."* I was learning what this verse meant for my situation.

***

Our supervisor, Mike Bush, was a fantastic team builder. Because of Mike's leadership, I began to feel a strong camaraderie with my coworkers. He encouraged a positive outlook on work and life, challenging us to serve the Lord whether at work or in the dorm.

The mood was light and we began to work as a team. We all gave each other nicknames and used them so much that, to this day, I forget some of their real names. One day, another dish pit guy and I were wearing Disney-themed shirts. His was Mickey Mouse and mine was, once again, Donald Duck. Everyone loved this coincidence, so from then on, it was, "Hey Donald!" and, "Hey Mickey!"

I learned that team bonding was vital when faced with challenges. The dish pit challenged all of us to win the daily battle of bitterness and discouragement. I could tell that most of us grew in the Lord by learning to interact more effectively with each other. Our comradery helped us work hard and laugh off our mistakes.

I was learning about friendship, and these experiences prepared me to meet Dan Bubar.

The Seriousness of Washing Mixing Bowls

Around the same time, a group of guys joined the kitchen: Eric Cordis, who became my roommate, and Dan who worked in the bakery. Dan's dad was part of the Word of Life staff, so his parents knew the crazy things that happened in the guys' dorms. Perhaps that was why Dan stayed at his grandmother's place for the summer. Every morning, he walked from town to work and then back again after his shift. So, I didn't see Dan except when our paths happened to cross at work.

Nevertheless, we formed a bond from the start of his first week. It was tiny, but it built a foundation for the following summer. I remember our first encounter. Picture a thin, small teenager with oversized glasses, dusted from head to toe in flour. The white spots on his apron proudly displayed evidence of his hard work, his hands were a sticky mess of chocolate, cream, and dough. The other bakers sent him on errands or tasked him with odd jobs; he was the go-to guy for any busy work, apparently because he was the youngest. I didn't know it yet, but he had only just turned 15, like me.

One fateful day, as I was diligently washing pots in the dish pit, Dan emerged from around the corner, clutching a sizable mixing bowl. He wore a look of urgency on his face and exclaimed, "Hey, I need this mixing bowl washed now! I'm serious!" His demands bubbled up laughter from the girls in the food prep area. No cook or baker had talked like this all summer, and the sight of this teen bemused most.

Unbeknownst to him, as he plopped the mixing bowl onto the black mat, his insistence became a subject of mockery for those observing. They were probably thinking, *Who does he think he is, barking orders like that and expecting instant obedience?* The sheer audacity of this newly minted 15-year-old demanding that we drop everything to clean a mixing bowl seemed absurd!

Mickey and I stood amidst towering piles of pots, pans, and utensils, sharing a knowing smirk.

"If you need it done so urgently," Mickey quipped, "why don't you wash it yourself?" Every cook and food prep person had something they needed within the next half hour or so; even in pressing situations, they wouldn't hesitate to roll up their sleeves and scrub it themselves.

So Mickey turned away in distain, "Yeah, right!" and resumed his vigorous scrubbing.

Meanwhile, Dan seemed to be in a state of utter panic. Alarm painted his face as he attempted to brush off the snickers and whispers from the sidelines, undoubtedly pondering what his next move would be in this intimidating game. His awkward boldness, though, brought a smile to my face.

Thoroughly entertained by this boy's audacity, I couldn't help myself. I reached out and took the mixing bowl from his hands. "All right," I declared, "I'll wash it for you." And with such a simple task, his severe and stressed look vanished as he looked at me with gratefulness. It marked the beginning of a riveting rollercoaster ride of navigating his amusingly stressful manner.

"Thank you." Smiling with a sense of accomplishment, he walked away to the bakery. Mickey disapproved, but I thought there might be an opportunity for kindness.

Once I finished washing the mixing bowl, I brought it around the corner to Dan. He appreciated my effort, and from that day on, I became his washing buddy. Whenever Dan needed something washed, he would bring it straight to me, knowing I would respect his request. Then, when I finished cleaning it, I would personally give it back to him.

After a while, I noticed Dan's job was to send the mixing bowls for washing. His fellow bakers, one of whom was Don Lough, Jr., likely sent him on these errands to provoke a smile. I always enjoyed my short visits to the bakery because I saw how kind and devoted the workers back there were—sometimes lingering for a small chat.

So Dan and I got to see each other more often, and I started to feel like we might be two sides of the same coin. We were both there to work for the Lord, even if it was grunt work, which it generally was since we were younger than the other staff. This small connection sparked our friendship.

Once summer ended, we were encouraged to recall what we had learned over the last couple of months. I thought about Colossians 3:23, *"Whatever you do, work heartily, as for the Lord and not for men."* Sometimes, it was hard to see how washing pots was a direct ministry for the Lord. Does someone get saved because I washed a pot? Yet, my contribution aided in many getting saved and being ministered to that summer.

Yet, having that verse in my mind reminded me to do every task, small or large, for the Lord. I could trust that God is the one who will work things out and use my service to him for his good. When I got home, I was not a perfect son, but these thoughts spurred me to do my best in the chores my mom assigned me. It was the foundation of a work ethic that I would continue to build upon as I learned more about God and who he is.

The Sly Fox

All the male staff stayed in the same dorm near the Island boat dock (Lodge B[7]). Dan, protected at his grandma's place in town, avoided some of the antics. Yet, I am sure he heard of some of them. Eric Cordis, his fellow Camper-in-Training taught us a few tricks. Around the middle of summer, the Camper-in-Training (CIT) spirit brought a new dimension to us all.[8]

When Dan was in his discipleship program, he met Eric Cordis, who had now become my roommate. This helped me hear about the summer fun they had together on the island. We were all in the kitchen: Dan was in the bakery, Eric was a cook, and I was a dishwasher.

That summer, water became a tool for revenge. The antics were rare at first, but they began happening more frequently after Eric Cordis joined our team halfway through the summer. He was always at the center of chaos, stirring things up. The discipleship program aimed for him to be a leader but I am not sure that they expected him to lead pranks and dorm battles.

During one of the water fights, Eric was given up as a human sacrifice to end the battle. Four guys carried him down to the dock despite his loud protests, and they unceremoniously dumped him into the lake. I would have felt bad since he was new, but he had already established a reputation for being a sly fox.

So it was no shock when my entire bed was soaked one night because of Eric Cordis. I share this story because I know many of you may have similar stories of misadventures at a WOL camp. Please feel free to identify with one of these characters…

At the beginning of the fight, I felt relatively safe, having put away my journal after writing a quick entry and preparing to wind down for my early shift the following day. One of the guys, let's call him Kyle, was talking loudly, but I knew he would quiet down soon to sleep, so I just ignored him. Eric, on the other hand, did not ignore him. Eric was one of the food line chefs and had early morning shifts, too, so Kyle's noise did not sit well with him.

Before I knew what was happening, Eric and Kyle started bantering and making light threats at each other until they were in the middle of the room, circling each other. I stared at them in annoyance, frustrated at their egos, and I wished for sleep. Our other roommate, Paul, was anything but annoyed. He looked on excitedly as things escalated, and he chimed in, "Eric, get the bucket! Get the bucket!"

A bucket of water was in the corner of our room, which we used as a quick defensive tactic. With the frequency of water fights at that point in the summer, we needed to be able to respond quickly to any attack. Everyone knew that access to the bathroom was prized and couldn't be relied on since it was the first place any layman would think of to get the proper armaments. A true water fighter knew to have a backup plan.

Eric ran over to grab the bucket, and Kyle grabbed the nearest thing that looked remotely threatening: shaving cream. Kyle gave a preliminary spray to taunt Eric and show the fierceness of his weapon. Eric stared at the stream of cream as it uneventfully landed on his big toe. Kyle looked disappointed and decided to let the full fury of the shaving cream unleash. He pushed the trigger, letting out an unrelenting stream of shaving cream at its fullest force. Eric got it good this time, but he quickly responded by lifting the dreaded bucket. Kyle taunted Eric, waggling his eyebrows and smirking at him, wordlessly daring him to throw the water. That was it. Eric quickly swung the bucket of water, aiming right at Kyle's smirking face.

Now, anyone who has ever thrown a bucket of water will have noticed Newton's laws of motion come into play. The first part of Newton's theory states that an object keeps moving until something stops it. The centripetal force will keep the water in the bucket until it stops swinging. Once it leaves the bucket, friction will slow it down, but in the case of water flying through air, the air presents negligible friction, so the water won't stop until it hits a target.

The second law states that the acceleration of water is determined in part by the force behind the object. With Kyle egging Eric on and Paul excitedly yelling from the sideline, Eric was definitely using a lot of force.

As a pro water-fighter, Eric should have known all these things, but at that moment, he made a rookie mistake. He didn't account for how the water would come out of the bucket much later than expected. So, as Kyle watched him swing the bucket of water towards him, he deftly moved aside, dodging the onslaught and clearing a pathway towards an alternate target. As the water left the bucket, it leaped through the air where Kyle had been just seconds before and headed straight for my bed. I'd been intending to relax and ignore the two and was lying on my bed, unaware of the coming baptism.

The third law of motion states that for every action, there is an equal and opposite reaction. Whatever that means, I reacted.

Shocked and thoroughly wet, I entered the moment's drama and yelled, "I cannot believe it! You messed up my bed, and it is totally wet! I cannot believe you did this! How could you do this!" My over-the-top yelling had achieved what I'd hoped: Ralph, the staff supervisor, entered the room to address the dilemma. If I had been a bit more mature, I could have laughed off the situation, but I confess that I made a big fuss then, hoping to force Ralph's hand to stop the endless water fights.

Ralph had been my roommate, but when Eric came, he moved downstairs to keep the boys calm. Lately, Ralph had handed out after-work hours to rambunctious teens who broke the rules. This time, he took my side.

Kyle and Eric faced extra work hours for the next ten days, which they had to do together. Rightly, their punishment involved water: they had to wash the kitchen and bakery floors, including the mats, at the end of each day. After a long day of work, no one was excited to clean up the floors, so it was the perfect punishment, especially since it excluded me. This "punishment" would mean less work for the dish pit, but they would see firsthand the mess in the bakery after a day of work. Eric brags to this day that the danishes were delicious at night.

Eric's friendship and fun encouraged me to seek out others who knew how to have a good time. This experience prepared me for the world of Dan Bubar, who sought clean fun at every turn. These guys, who knew how to have fun, yet were also spiritually aware, were natural magnets to me as an introvert.

My summer friendships and learning to serve the Lord from the heart encouraged me to stay in my public school. I wanted to continue the few friendships I had there. The summer gave me some tools to encourage other believers and the courage to witness. This became a good way to serve the Lord from the heart since I realized that many I knew did not know the Lord.

Eric and Dan - Is that a Danish you are eating, Eric?

Chapter Three - The Burning Bakery of 1982

After such a fun, full 1981 summer of companionship in the dish pit, I hoped to recreate some of those memories the following summer. When I decided which job I wanted, I again chose dish pit. I suppose I was a glutton for punishment because most people didn't willingly choose dish pit.

To most people, the dish pit evoked images of a hot kitchen with tedious scrubbing, wrinkled fingers, and soaked clothes: a liquid covering their whole body, and nobody knew which was from the dishes and which was sweat. It's not a pleasant picture, especially considering how teen boys usually smell when they sweat. Yet, the dish pit was a place of comradery. So, when I landed my dream job, I was elated and ready to work wholeheartedly alongside some new friends.

Before work could start, there was a summer kickoff where all the staff would head to the Island for a meal and a message. It was a time to get excited about the summer and to connect with new people. Those who had worked the previous summer would use this time to reconnect, which is precisely what I did. As I got in line for food, I noticed Eric Cordis' head bobbing in the crowd. Dan Bubar was by his side, and I waved at them. They were further back in line, and I stood with no one I knew. With their wave, I felt accepted and quickly headed back towards them. I was excited to see the familiar faces. Seeing anyone you know, even slightly, in a large crowd can be comforting.

Naturally, we started talking about the previous summer, reminiscing about all the odd and crazy things. A rehearsal of *get-the-bucket* found its way into recollections and, to Dan's chagrin concerning the loss of some nightly danishes by Eric, this meal was a time full of excitement and reconnection. I was sure I hadn't made a lasting impression on Dan the previous summer, since we'd only discussed surface-level things. However, I wanted to get to know him better and knew that spending time with him would be enjoyable. His excitement rubbed off on me, and I felt encouraged by his personality.

As we sat together after the meal at the staff campfire, he shared stories of commitment on that spot. He seemed serious-minded and one who could make a good friend. With him, if we became friends, I knew I could find someone to grow together in my faith and, when needed, to share my inner thoughts and struggles. Still, as the next week of work went by, we only acknowledged each other and had light-hearted conversations despite him working in the bakery — the most secluded place in the kitchen. Something more may come of this, I thought.

The Life-Altering Moment

At the end of the first week of the summer of 1982, Paul Dilger, one of the head chefs, walked over to me as I put a tray of dishes into the dishwasher.[9]

"How are you liking dish pit?"

"Oh, I love it. I am so glad I got placed here; it was my first choice." I loved the dish pit, but I also wanted to ensure the chefs knew I was cheerful in my work. Paul seemed a little shocked at my response. He expected less enthusiasm since dish pit is the least coveted job.

"Well, I'm glad you're enjoying this job, but there's an area in the kitchen that needs a little help right now, and I think you'd enjoy working there too."

So, when Paul Dilger came to me and said these words, I frowned inwardly, feeling a sense of doom settled over me at the thought of leaving the camaraderie of the dish pit. Paul continued, "You see, Dan Bubar is alone in the bakery right now, and he mentioned that you two were buddies and you would fit the role perfectly."

I felt honored that Dan thought so highly of me, but something was off. "I thought there were two people assigned to the bakery. Did the other never show up?"

"He was working with Dan for the first week," Paul responded, and then added cryptically, "but he is no longer working there." Hmm. I nodded, deeming it best not to ask why. I remembered moments when I felt cheerful at work and decided to maintain a positive attitude, even if it meant taking on a new role. I wanted to be open to serving where needed, whether in the bakery or the dish pit.

"I am willing to switch if needed there," I said firmly.

"Thank you. I know Dan will appreciate your help." Paul smiled at me and walked away, ready to inform my supervisor about the decision.

I looked towards the entryway to the bakery corner and felt a twinge of sadness, thinking of the seclusion around that corner. I had no idea this new assignment would bring me one of the most incredible opportunities for comradery.

Paul returned a few minutes later and handed me a fresh white apron. I removed my dish pit apron and waved slightly to the guys in the pit before following Paul back to the bakery. Dan greeted me warmly, and we worked together for the rest of the shift.

That night, in my journal, I wrote, "*June 29, 1982- It is sad to leave [the dish pit], but it is what the Lord wants.*" My initial hesitation was not an aversion to Dan since I liked him. It was only because I enjoyed working as a team with a group of guys. However, the tradeoff brought along an unexpected lifelong friend. We were about to embark on the best summer two teenagers could experience in a workplace. If I could ever relive that time, I would.

***

I wrote this about my first morning with Dan:

"June 30, 1982-Today I got up at 5:30 am and was the second one into the kitchen. Dan and I made quite a lot of things and it was fun. The morning went really smoothly, and we got out at 12:30 and then went back at 3:30 pm. Tonight, we made Pumpkin Pies, and they were good."

The *smoothness* that I mentioned didn't last for long. We soon called ourselves "The Bubar/Butler Burning Bakery, or the BBB bakery for short. Based on my journal, we expected to burn things; from day one, I labeled our time at the work as the B & B Burning Bakery in my journal, even though we didn't burn anything. Bubar (what I called him mostly) was known for his absent-mindedness, and from the beginning, I joined in on this by forgetting what we were baking.

We seemed to burn puddings, cookies, bread products — nothing was beyond us. We would be excited about our ability to make the products quickly and efficiently, so by the time we placed them in the oven, our excitement led us to think the process was complete and then we forgot about it. Once something was in the oven, it was out of sight and out of mind. It was too late when the acrid scent of burning food reached our noses. Usually, it wasn't so late that Dan and I couldn't munch on the cookies or whatever we

23

burned. So, I'm sure mankind was richer when we offered the tray of partially burned cookies to the other staff or popped a few in our mouths.

We joked that the burnt food was our burnt offerings to God. That made us feel better, but after so many times, we needed a solution. We tried putting a colored towel on the oven handle to remind us when something was inside, but even then, time would get the best of us, passing more quickly with each moment of laughter and conversation. Eventually, Dan brought in an alarm clock from his grandma Ebba Swanson's place to help us remember the items in the oven.[10] Not surprisingly, without the burnt cookies filling us up, we both felt hungrier when lunch arrived.

Another struggle we had was with the donut machine. At first, I liked making donuts with Dan, but the machine often malfunctioned. Close monitoring and refilling of the dough were needed every few minutes. Ideally, the donut machine was supposed to be automatic and require little effort from us. Yet, time and time again, the moving rack would move too fast or too slow, ruining the donut shape or placing one on top of another. Or the donut-cutting contraption would cut the donuts too small. Most of the time, we ended up with oddly shaped donuts or donuts that were stuck together. We still served them to the guests, and they seemed to enjoy them. In the end, a donut is a donut, and most people love them, but for Dan and me, they represented a minor failure.

Near the end of our shift one day, Dan and I were wallowing in dread of the next morning. We knew we would have to make donuts, and we were already anxious about the probability of the donut machine's impending antics.

"Butler, I have an idea," Dan said, immediately brightening up. I laughed at his sudden excitement, unable to imagine anything to fix the machine's issues. "I'm serious!" Dan continued.

"You're always saying you're serious." I responded, rolling my eyes, "How serious are you?" Because the only thing I can imagine that would make making donuts easier is if I didn't have to make them at all.

"I *am* serious." Dan glared at me, clearly annoyed, "You are not getting out of it that easily, but maybe we could make the process less stressful if you just listen to my idea." I stared at him expectantly, urging him to continue, "Well, maybe we can take turns coming in early to start up the machine and get the dough ready. Then, we can test the machine to identify the malfunction that has occurred, and we can have more time to help it out without the added stress of manual intervention.

"That probably would help…" I paused, thinking of missing an extra hour or so of sleep, "but I don't want to take the first turn. Since you made the plan, you should do it first." I paused again as he looked at me suspiciously. "That way, you can show me the best way to do it," I continued quickly, hoping to hide my selfishness.

Dan smiled at me graciously, looking right through my facade, but he nodded in agreement. "When you arrive at work, I will update you on the situation, and we can develop a plan of action."

The following day, Dan kept his word. As soon as we exchanged our "good mornings," he gave me an update on the donut machine. Things went more smoothly than usual, which wasn't saying much, but we were glad we could adapt to alleviate the burden, even if only slightly.

Making donuts throughout the summer taught us the value of patience. The following week, it was my turn to take the earlier shift for the donuts. I did all the necessary preparations and felt quite accomplished once Dan arrived. I updated him on the situation, and we started making donuts. However, it wasn't long before a stream of smoke began to rise from the oil. This was new. Dan and I shared a confused look, but we didn't get anxious, panicky, or frustrated. God was helping us make the best of the situation, even if it seemed complicated.

"Do you think it's because the machine got cleaned yesterday?" I asked.

"Maybe…" Dan stared as the smoke began to expand. "It could just be burning off some of the chemicals… maybe it will stop soon." I nodded quickly, hoping he was right. We continued working, but suddenly, the smoke alarm started to blare. Our eyes widened, and Dan ran over to the alarm, trying to fan it so it would turn off. It was too late; we heard a booming voice around the corner.

"Bubar!" the head chef called out. What did you burn this time?" Bubar was the target of the trouble, and I seemed to escape the rap; yet I was just as much to blame.

"Nothing is burning," I interjected quickly. "The oil is just smoking a bit. We were hoping it would stop soon." I looked at the chef expectantly while Bubar continued to fan at the alarm frantically.

"What kind of oil did you put in there? The only reason it would be smoking like this is if you put in an oil with a low smoking point." The chef reached up and casually pressed a button to stop the alarm. Dan looked embarrassed but also relieved to be able to stop fanning the air like a madman. Meanwhile, I started absorbing his anxiety as I realized that it was my fault that the oil was smoking. I must have put in the wrong oil.

"I put in the oil earlier and thought it was right, but maybe not…" I trailed off. The chef walked over to one of the finished donuts and took a bite. Dan and I looked expectantly at him, while the smoke snuck closer to the alarm again.

"Yep," the chef said with surety. They taste a little different, so it must be a different oil. They still taste fine, though. At this point, the oil is too hot to change, so finish up the batch you're on, and then we will turn off the machine to let the oil cool. We can change the oil once it's cooled down." We nodded at him and continued our work once he left.

The alarm went off numerous times after that, and each time, the chef would promptly come around the corner to turn it off. And Dan became progressively more annoyed with my mistake each time it occurred. Luckily, we eventually laughed about it, especially in light of all the other errors we made that summer.

Bubar Pranks?!

God empowered us to look past the stress, and we knew He would get us through it all, even while we joked around. Bubar allowed me to take life less seriously with his practical jokes.

Over the window in our bakery, a little plaque said: "Superpretzel loves you!" with a smiling pretzel hugging the words "loves you." This became our mantra to encourage one another.

The bakery was located at the edge of the kitchen, near the loading dock, and a walkway to the storage sheds was visible from our two windows.[11] We saw people walking toward the alleyway near the sheds from one of the windows. Our other window was above that alleyway, but we couldn't see out of it since it was higher up. For fun, we sometimes yelled to someone we knew, "Hey, Superpretzel loves you!" as we saw them walk by the side window. At times, if it were a friend like Eric Cordis, we would always have a cup of water ready. As he entered the alleyway near the sheds, one of us would throw the cup of water out the window and onto his head. We always relished the inevitable gasp of shock. Eric wasn't our only beneficiary. We blessed others with a cup of cold water. Usually, the first-time recipients would have no idea where the water came from because the window was so high up. However, occasionally, our snickering gave us away, and they'd know that it was the Bubar/Butler Burning Bakery up to no good again.

One glorious time, we had the chance to expand our clever trick. The head chef always seemed to clash with Dan. Since Dan was a local kid, he worked in the kitchen during the school year too, so they had a rocky relationship after spending so much time together. As a teen with a big responsibility, Dan was prone to making mistakes, which the chef started calling "Bubar's Blunders." It didn't help that our title, "The Bubar/Butler Burning Bakery," was well-known throughout the kitchen. Whenever Dan heard the chef raising his voice, "Bubar!" he would start dreading the expected reprimand.

The chef had every right to be angry at our antics and teenage tomfoolery, but we were most likely his daily trial.

One day, we had a three-hour training session with food director Burt Powell.[12] We were trying to master new recipes. That day, the bakery corner got sweltering. We had our small window open above our heads and the corner window at the side, letting in fresh air, but it didn't alleviate the heat much.

As a seasoned baker, Burt was bearing with the heat, but Dan and I were struggling, continually drinking cups of ice water. While Dan was sipping his cup, I let Burt in on our secret, "You know what we use these cups for sometimes?" Burt looked at me quizzically, and I continued, "Sometimes, when we see someone about to pass by the alleyway, we fill a cup with water and splash it on them. It's great because they can't see us and have no idea where it's coming from."

Burt started laughing loudly while Dan and I continued to drink our water.

"Well, I want to see that; let's get a cup ready with extra water to toss on someone." Dan and I looked at each other, shocked, but we quickly readied a cup, excited to add some shenanigans to our three hours in the heat. Not long after that, we saw the head chef walking towards the alleyway.

"Dan, grab the cup of water!" Burt called out. Dan giddily grabbed the water and waited for Burt to signal before throwing it out the window. Suddenly, we heard the chef yell out, "Bubar!" We looked at each other nervously, but Burt laughed, clearly enjoying the venture.

Moments later, the chef came around the corner, ready to scold Bubar. When he saw Burt, his boss, he seemed shocked. Burt stood there, chuckling.

"Hey, Chef, how was that?" Did you enjoy the baptism? Wasn't that funny?" Burt continued to snicker as he spoke. The chef gave a tight-lipped smirk at Burt and walked away without a word. Dan and I were laughing at our luck. Even after that day, we reminisced about how hilarious that situation was (obviously exaggerating it more and more every time). We still couldn't believe that Burt would do that, but I guess there is a little boy in every man's heart.

I'm sure that day didn't improve Dan's reputation in the head chef's eyes. As the summer progressed, the tension between them became comical because there were so many things in our folly we tried to "fix," but they all ended in horrible disasters, and the head chef seemed to witness every single one!

Bakery and Burning Challenges

A challenge we consistently faced was making Danish pastries. Danishes required a lot of precision and time, so burning even one tray significantly limited us since we had a quota to reach. We took great care not to burn them, hoping to have extras to snack on. We both loved danishes, but the time and effort required for them made any extra snacking almost impossible.

Every time we ruined a tray of goodies; we sought to hide the issue. It was easier to hide our mistakes than to confront the head chef about our shortcomings, yet inevitably, a chef would find us out and usually discover our mistakes. Since we hid them, he was usually more annoyed. It would have been better for us to be honest and humble about our mistakes, but instead, we were pushed along by the fear of man.

One time, hiding our mistake for too long had dire consequences. We were making Baked Alaskas. These Alaskas were made from a cake layer with four towering scoops of ice cream, later covered with meringue. Usually, the kitchen was so hot that we would scoop the ice cream in the freezer to prevent it from melting. Although this led to numb fingers, it was the easy part of the process.

The true challenge was the meringue that was supposed to be laid atop the ice cream. Back then, we didn't realize that humidity was the probable culprit of our meringue struggles. Humidity can hinder the meringue from getting thick and stiff, and New York summers were quite humid — especially in a hot kitchen. We hated making the meringue because we never knew when it would cooperate or why it sometimes didn't.

As we made the meringue that day, we realized it was taking longer than usual.

"This needs to stiffen up soon. Maybe something is wrong?" Dan said.

We continued to work on the meringue, but as time passed and it did not form anything close to a stiff peak, we decided to change our plan.

"Let's add some cream of tartar. That might help stabilize it." Dan said confidently. I grabbed the cream of tartar and added some. As we continued to work on it, our dread grew with each minute that it stayed flat and liquid. At that point, we should have told somebody of our struggles, but as pride often does, it made us reluctant to ask for help, and we didn't want to face the disappointment of the chefs.

So, we tried to handle things on our own. We quickly started to make another meringue, hoping it would stiffen up...It failed too!

"Bubar, what should we do?" I stared at the limp white liquid before us.

"We should probably tell somebody..." Dan responded with a sigh, clearly looking stressed.

"Or we could put whipped cream on the Alaskas and pretend it's meringue," I joked, trying to lighten the mood. Dan gave a quick chuckle before I continued, "I'm too intimidated to tell the main chef. Who knows how he will react? Maybe we can pull Chef Dilger aside and tell him." Dan nodded quickly, and I hurried around the corner to get Chef Paul Dilger.

He regarded our two bowls of unimpressive meringue.

"I wish you guys had told me sooner; we could have done something about this mess. At this point, though..." Paul sighed and rubbed his forehead, "We don't have enough time before the meal starts. We will have to serve something else. Let me speak with the chef briefly to determine what to serve." As Paul walked away, we felt guilty that we couldn't serve the guests the Alaskas, which were usually a crowd favorite. We were also relieved that we wouldn't have to face the head chef directly. That summer helped me handle confrontation a bit better, but even now, it remains a struggle.

Eventually, Paul returned to inform us that he and the chef had decided to serve the guests ice cream sundaes. The Alaskas taught us to be forthcoming with our struggles because being humble and accepting help when offered is better than stubbornly holding on to pride and making a fool of yourself. It is like the verse, *"Whoever exalts himself will be humbled, and whoever humbles himself will be* exalted" (Matt. 23:12 ESV). We were making innocent mistakes, so we had no reason to dread being forthcoming about them. God continued to humble and sanctify us so that we might represent Him better.

On one occasion, we put the coffee cakes in the oven and then leisurely went to breakfast. The intention was to return in time to take them out, but time got the best of us as we continued talking. We had completely forgotten about the coffee cakes until the chef stormed into our breakfast area, quite dismayed. He had rescued the coffee cakes since they were on the verge of a complete disaster but muttered about putting us in the dish pit. Our young, delinquent baking was a frustration to many.

Dan and I would almost ruin something, but the head chef would save it before it was unservable to guests. In a sense, he was keeping us from the familiar shame of ruining the guests' dessert. Instead of making a different dessert like with the Alaskas, his watchful eye in the kitchen spared us on many occasions. The head chef helped us realize the responsibility we had. We couldn't always rely on someone else to take something out before it burned. Yet, that day, we took a longer break than usual, shirking our other responsibilities. As two 15-year-old boys, it was hard to realize the weight of our duties and the direct consequences of shirking them, even for a moment.

***

Besides learning to burn things, I learned how to bake things properly. I had thought I already knew how to bake well since I occasionally made cookies and cakes at home, but it was very different from learning to bake in the Inn bakery. Everything we made was in bulk, so we used pounds and ounces instead of the measurements I was familiar with, such as cups and tablespoons. Some recipes would even call for more than ten pounds of flour, so you can see why we couldn't be measured in cups.

With so many ingredients and weighing involved, following the recipe closely, from start to finish, was essential. Even weighing one ingredient incorrectly could throw off the whole recipe. This was quite a challenge because, even at home, I could easily forget how many cups of flour I had used.

Dan started a dinner roll recipe, but something came up, and I was required to finish it. I think he told me he had measured half of half of the total recipe (1/4), but I heard him say he had done half the recipe. So, I looked in the flour bowl and somehow decided I needed to add half the amounts, doubling the required salt and yeast. Honestly, to this day, I don't know exactly what went wrong, but either way, it was my fault.

After I set the dough aside to proof, Dan returned and checked on it. We noticed it was expanding rapidly, and Dan looked at me worried.

"Butler…what did you do? At this rate, it will get everywhere."

"I don't know; I think I followed the recipe correctly. Let me taste it." I pulled out a tiny piece of dough and put it in my mouth as Dan watched expectantly. "Blegh!" I spat the dough out into a nearby trash can and started laughing. "Bubar," I coughed between words, "I just made the saltiest dough I've ever tasted." Dan tried a tiny bite, too, and began to choke and laugh as well.

"We're supposed to be the Bubar-Butler Burning Bakery, not the ruin-it-before-you-can-even-bake-it bakery." Dan said, to which I replied, "Well, at least we can't burn it because we can't even bake it!" We laughed nervously as we both realized we had made an inedible and emerging blob.

"It might not be completely ruined," I said brightly, "If we fix the ratios, maybe we can salvage it."

Dan stared at me incredulously, "Butler, it's too late for that! We have to start the whole recipe over!" He waited while I took this in. "I'm serious."

"Well, we can't just throw it away. What if it expands out of the trash can and all over the bakery?" We looked at each other as we thought it through.

"Well…" Dan started, "if we put it in the fridge, that will slow it down until we figure out what to do with it." I brightened. I was eager to have the offensive blob out of sight while we made its replacement. I didn't want anyone asking. Dan and I grabbed the dough container and placed it inconspicuously near the back of the walk-in fridge.

We started making the new dough to make up for lost time. Anytime I heard the door of the walk-in click shut, I would feel tense, expecting someone to walk around the corner and confront us with our mistake. However, after a whole shift passed without anyone mentioning a thing, I started to relax. The new dough was done, and the old dough had escaped detection.

To our young minds, the solution seemed obvious: leave it where it is, and nobody will notice. Dan and I had heard many Word of Life sermons about doing our work unto the Lord and not unto men, but fear of man won out, and we hid our mistake. Adam and Eve had fig leaves, and we had a big walk-in fridge.

The inevitable happened. A few days later, the head chef came to our corner. He started the conversation with, "I love you in the Lord, but…" Then he led us to the walk-in fridge and pointed at the dough. It had oozed out of its container, covering the shelf with sticky tendrils. Guilt and embarrassment overwhelmed us. We both apologized for the mess and told him what had happened, including the dumb choice we made. Honesty had proven challenging to live out, especially when it made us look bad. But even if others were disappointed or judgmental, we began to see that God's opinion mattered more, and the chef forgave us. It was a picture of Christ, who declares us righteous before God, even when we mess up.

Eventually, near the end of the summer, the head chef called me into his office, and my (then 16-year-old) teenage mind was given some perspective. He talked to me like a friend, helping me see that even those in authority are like the rest of us. I was thankful for that time. I noticed that he was a man with a whole life outside of being a chef and wanted to serve the guests to the best of his ability. It taught me not to fight authority but to see that they intend to encourage. I didn't know it then, but it also impacted me in the future, as I want to remain approachable in leadership positions.

The next day, the head chef brought me a Donald Duck mug because he had known my nickname from the previous summer. It was a small gesture, but it touched my heart because he had remembered such a small detail about my life. From then on, I no longer felt intimidated by him. Later, as Dan continued to work with and around the chef, his intimidation of him slowly dissipated. They even later served together in their local church and became good friends.

For us, the summer antics became a thing to laugh about together as we reminisced about our teenage fear of what we thought was a stern chef. Our bakery stories were exaggerated through embellishments to portray our innocent chef as the antagonist. In reality, we came to appreciate him in many ways for the lessons he taught us. He was doing his job as a chef, and we must have frustrated him.

***

Messiness is not close to Godliness

Dan had a reputation for being incredibly messy. I had already known this from my first encounter with him the previous summer, and being in the bakery, I witnessed it firsthand. Typically, people thought all our messes were Dan's fault. One time, however, we finally had a scapegoat.

Many of our recipes called for an extravagant amount of flour, which we were supposed to mix slowly in the automatic mixing bowl. We saw firsthand what happens when flour is mixed in on a faster setting.

We were running behind on the banana bread, so one of the STC cooks came over to help us. Dan mixed the wet ingredients in the large, automatic mixer while I measured out the 10 pounds of flour. Once Dan finished, I poured in the flour. It was ready for the slow stirring process. The young cook, eager to help, turned on the mixer to the third speed, hoping to finish the dough quickly for the sake of time. Before Dan and I could let out a warning, flour flew all over the small bakery. The cook promptly turned off the mixer, but by then, heaps of flour had spewed out in every direction.

The cook looked at us sheepishly, and we all laughed hysterically at the absurdity of the situation. We started to clean up, but soon the cook was called back to work, and Dan and I were left with an unforgettable mess. We were relieved that at least our baking corner was tiny and probably wouldn't take long to clean up. As time passed, though, there seemed to be minimal improvement. The flour was on us, under our shoes, and still all over the floor. To make things worse, we had to keep working, and whenever we walked back and forth from food prep to the bakery, we left flour footprints all over the black mats.

We realized the whole kitchen would discover our

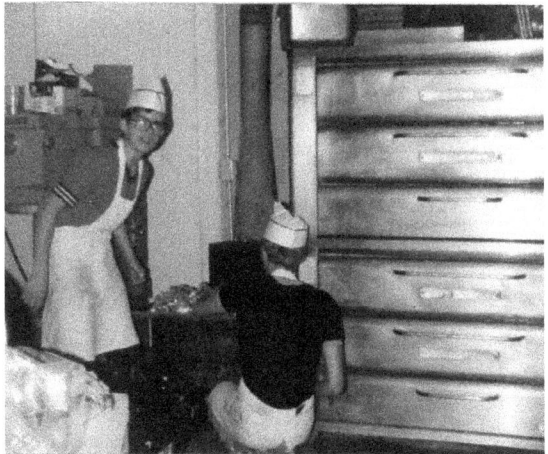

Dan & I fixing Swan Cream Puffs - the menu for each Saturday

flour fiasco since our footprints were everywhere. Soon, various staff members from all the different areas of the kitchen came to our corner to witness the destruction. They either laughed at us or laughed with us.

Other than the hilarity of the situation, we were posed with a problem more significant than a mess: what do you do with a bowl of batter when an unknown amount of flour flies out of it? How can we determine the amount of flour to add to the bowl? Luckily, one of the chefs, Paul Dilger, came to the rescue. His kitchen wisdom often proved invaluable.

He mixed the dough and felt it with his hands. Quietly, he added some more flour, seemingly a random amount, yet something in his mind or his fingers was calculating how much flour the dough needed. Dan and I watched in amazement as he slowly fixed the dough. His familiarity with his work allowed him to adapt to this unusual situation. He didn't just rely on a list of directions; he had internalized the work to the point of understanding the "why" behind each ingredient in the recipe, allowing him to adjust things due to his greater understanding. I noticed that this

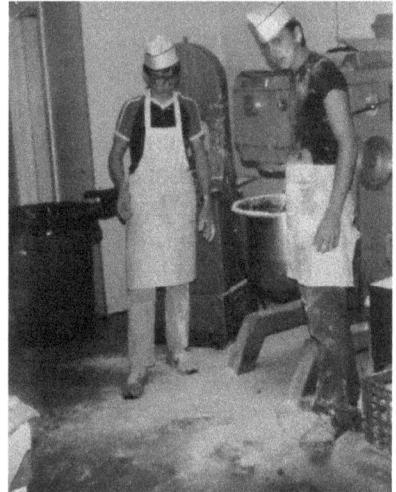

The result of the flour and the mixer

was a superior way of doing work, regardless of the task.

A Hot Mess

Most of Dan's messiness was the constant smattering of flour covering his apron, but once, he expanded his skills to the sink. He needed to thaw a large tub of whipped frosting, so he began filling the sink with hot water and placed the tub inside. To do this, he had to fill the sink considerably, so he turned on the tap and intended to let it fill while he tended to other tasks.

Around the time the water was full enough, Dan was still busy doing other things, so even though the sink was right behind him in the tiny bakery, he didn't notice his predicament. The sink began to overflow. As water started pouring onto the floor, Dan turned around frantically and reached to turn off the water.

"Butler! You have to help me!" I peeked around the corner and laughed at his anxious expression..

"Butler!" Dan said hurriedly, "You have to empty this sink! I'm busy with the Danishes! I'm serious!" Still chuckling, I sauntered towards the crime scene.

"How did you forget about the sink? It's right there," I said, reaching my hand in to pull the plug.

"It already happened. Let's not dwell on the how; let's figure this out," Dan responded.

But as soon as my fingers touched the water, I yanked back my hand.

"Ouch!" I held my fingers close to my body. "Dan, that water is boiling!" Dan began to see the humor in the situation.

"I guess we just have to let it cool down then," Dan smirked as I grimaced in pain. I nodded, annoyed with myself for not testing the water. I got a gallon pail and began scooping out the water, running it to the Food Prep sink and dumping it out. After a few minutes of this crazed, one-man relay, I ran cold water into the sink. Eventually, the water was cool enough to drain and refill to a safe level. Besides that and the occasional water fight, we didn't have too many water-related messes.

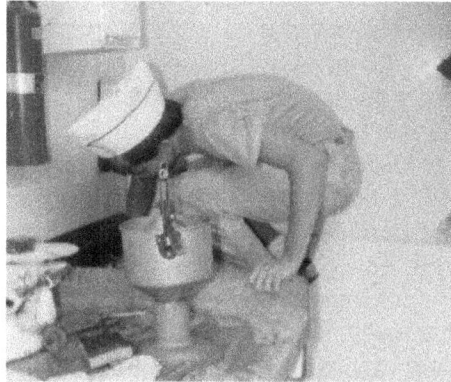

Attempting to pull the plug in the sink

The bottom line was that when Dan focused on something, he forgot about everything else. You could never accuse him of not working hard, though. If someone came out of a day's work in the bakery with nothing on their apron, they'd either done nothing or performed a miracle. Even Glenn Slothower, the head baker at the Ranch and later Food Director, was known for his meticulous attention to detail. He said it took him two years of challenging himself before he could make trays of brownies with icing without a single spot on his apron. Some of us are driven in different directions for different reasons. Dan and I never took on that type of challenge.

Eventually, Dan's reputation for being messy spread to me. One day, after a perfect flour fight, someone approached me and remarked, "You look as bad as Dan." I wasn't too worried about the comment since that summer had taught me that cleanliness is *not* next to godliness.

But God did want us to learn responsibility. For years, Food Director Burt Powell's words echoed in our conversations: An inch is a cinch, but a yard is hard. He often helped us learn new baking techniques and noticed how messy we were. He looked at the bakery bench and said those famous words, meaning that each inch of the wooden counter needed to be cleaned consistently and continually. His words of wisdom intrigued our young minds.

Once, he entered the bakery, stared at our pile of dirty dishes in the sink, and moved his eyes to the cluttered counter, quipping, "Clean as you go, or you go." He then showed us some examples of cleaning as you go while we watched this new phenomenon. Despite what our moms may have thought; we did try to implement this new standard of cleaning into our lives. We ensured our counter space was clean before starting a new recipe. Burt helped us a lot, yet Dan's apron remained a collage of ingredients, and his reputation for messiness never changed. You may even have heard the famous Steve Bubar quote regarding Dan: "You have it from your ear to your rear and your nose to your toes."

Yet, despite our many mishaps, we worked hard that summer and grew closer to one another and the Lord. In the following years, Dan was a messy example to the new staff, encouraging them to keep clean rather than a mess. People in charge could laugh at Dan's messiness because he was hard-working and passionate about his work.

Speed and Competition

Dan was speedy as well. He strived to do things quickly and efficiently; sometimes, this led to mistakes, but other times, it made him proficient. One thing that we both enjoyed making was sticky buns. We would make it into a race to see who could finish knotting them first. We had to make about 300 to 400 sticky buns each Friday, so we had plenty of opportunities to compete. We usually started with 36 pieces of dough each. Each dough piece had to be rolled out and tied before being added to the pile.

Dan and I would make the first round of tying a practice round. It was a simple warm-up to prepare for the upcoming competition. Then, we would prepare the next round of dough pieces for the genuine race.

"You ready, Bubar?" I asked him, with our individual 36 untied dough pieces before us.

Dan wiggled his fingers, "More ready than you. GO!" Dan quickly started rolling out the dough. I raced to catch up with his millisecond lead. Though knot quality was essential to us both, it tended to move down the priority list if the competitor was getting too far ahead.

"Done!" Dan exclaimed as he threw the last piece of dough on the pile. I quickly tossed in my last piece right after him.

"How many seconds was that?" I asked Dan. He grabbed the stopwatch.

"40 seconds," he said proudly.

"Now, let me look at your pile..." I said, edging over to examine his dough knots. Dan confidently scoffed at my scrutiny.

"Ha!" I exclaimed, holding up a suspiciously tied knot, "Is this Word of Life quality?" Dan grabbed the knot in disdain.

"Oh, c'mon, it looks better than half the knots in your pile." He fished one out for proof. Despite their questionable appearance, every sticky bun made it to the pan.

"How will the guest know if the knot is bad after baking?"

"Butler, they have mine to compare it to. That's how they will know," Dan replied in fake seriousness.

After many races of similar fashion, we decided to make the competition even more challenging by starting with 72 pieces. We felt this would be the true test of speed and efficiency. Dan won the race, but half the knots were truly questionable, and they worsened as the weighty dough became a sticky, knotted pile. Ultimately, it showed us that we couldn't have

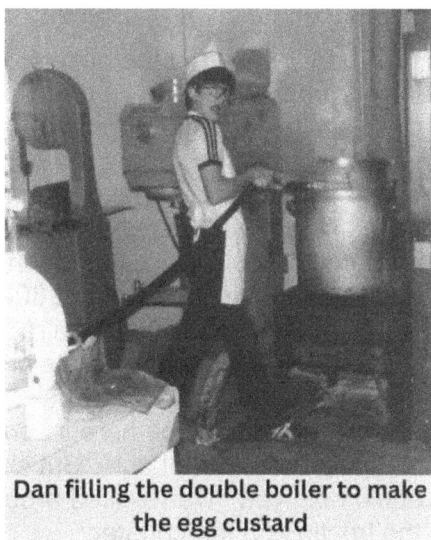

Dan filling the double boiler to make the egg custard

both quality and speed when it came to sticky buns.

We wisely decided to stick with 36-piece races, maintaining the quality while still having fun.

Kicked into the Dorm

Dan and I had more adventures together, even outside the kitchen, because eventually, he joined dorm life. As the son of a staff member, Dan initially stayed in the comforts of his home in town or at his grandma's house while working at the Inn. He either walked or rode his bike up to the Inn. The rest of the summer staff were stuck in the dorms with two-inch-thick mattresses (if you could call them that) and rickety bed frames. I didn't mean to, but I think I accidentally got Dan moved into the dorms at midsummer.

On my day off, one of the teen chefs woke me up at 6:40 am. I looked at him with my eyes half closed, confused and panicked. *Was I supposed to work today?* Before I could ask a question, he informed me that Dan hadn't arrived at work yet, and he was supposed to be there by 6:15, so they needed me to go in. I'd become the default since the morning chef didn't know where Dan lived. I got ready and dragged my feet to the kitchen, hoping the brisk morning walk would shake off my grogginess. I imagined Dan accidentally sleeping in, probably because his bed was so comfy, but I wasn't mad at him. I was surprised, though, because he was usually punctual.

When I arrived at the bakery, I turned on the light and took some icing from the fridge to let it soften, which we would later drizzle over the biscuits. Usually, Dan made the biscuits, and I did the icing, so I was pretty clueless about the process. With every tick of the clock, I was reminded that I had to prepare several trays of biscuits with only a little more than an hour before the guests started arriving.

Before I could panic too much, Dan showed up. He looked calm and collected as if he weren't 30 minutes or so late for work.

"Dan, I am so relieved you're here!"

"And I'm so shocked you're here," he responded with a laugh. "Isn't it your day off?"

"Well, I wouldn't be here if *someone* hadn't slept in," I joked while slapping him on the back. "But since I'm here already, I guess I could help you." Dan looked around at the empty bakery and eyed the frosting on the counter.

"Yeah… It appears that you've made significant progress without my help. And I didn't sleep in. I can make all the biscuits before eight like I need to, without losing an hour of sleep. Watch me and see how I do it, and maybe you, too, can save your precious sleep."

He then proceeded to gather all the ingredients for the biscuits. He mixed, rolled, and cut them, then popped them in the oven. From start to finish, he took around 45 minutes. The freshly baked biscuits would be served warm. I was shocked, but I was glad I got to witness a world record, or maybe just a Word of Life record. I was impressed by Dan's expertise and preparedness in his work. He performed his role effortlessly, and I aspired to reach that level.

I'm not sure if this "crisis" got him moved to the dorms, but I'm glad he did. On day one, I decided to visit his room, since it was next door. When I walked in, he was working intensely on something.

"Hey, Bubar. What are you up to?" I asked.

Dan glanced over quickly and responded, "Oh, it's nothing. Just writing… you know." He continued to scratch away with his pen. I started to walk closer out of curiosity, and I saw Dan instinctively hover a hand over his work, trying to hide it.

"Bubar!" I exclaimed as I saw the edge of the Word of Life Quiet Time book below his hand. "Why are you working on the quiet time from three days ago?" I looked expectantly at him, already having an inkling of his answer.

"Well…" Dan started, looking for an excuse. I waited, raising my eyebrows at him and smiling.

"Ugh, fine." He continued reluctantly, "I haven't done my quiet time this week, and my supervisor said he would check to see if I'm doing them. If I'm not, I can't go off campus. It's ironic because I lived off campus before today." He sighed and looked down, ashamed. "Jeff, I even tried showing him an older week of quiet time, and he caught me red-handed. It was embarrassing." Amused, I took advantage as a teen buddy.

"WOW!" I shook my head. "Your dad develops the quiet time books," I said exaggeratedly, "and his son doesn't do them! Who would've thought?"

"Butler, you can't tell anyone this. I'm serious." Suddenly concerned, he looked at me wide-eyed, and I nodded. Oops. I guess I broke my word by writing this now, but my excuse is that he used the phrase "I'm serious" so often that he probably wasn't serious 50% of the time, and we'll toss this story into that 50%.

In reality, everyone is human and struggles in their righteous deeds. Yet even those are filthy rags before God; so, thank God we have Christ to cover us with His righteousness. Perhaps that situation taught Dan not to do things for show but rather to do them for God, who graces us with infinite opportunities. Without the suffocating weight of trying to achieve righteousness before others, but rather resting in Christ's grace, Dan remained consistent with his quiet time throughout the many years I knew him.

Our self-discipline in our daily time with God created a vision for our lives. Despite our struggles at times, we knew how to push each other to ponder what God had for us each day and view things through His eyes rather than our own.

In ministry overseas, this becomes one of the areas of inquiry for those short-termers who visit our fields. What are you doing for a daily devotional time? Many struggle with daily time or use devotionals but do not read the Scripture. Word of Life taught Dan and me that this was foundational to knowing God's will for our lives.

Dan's Love for the Island

One summer, before Dan had moved to "the barracks," he discovered a new phenomenon. We were standing near the beach, and suddenly, Dan and I heard screams and cheering in the distance. We realized the sound was traveling across the water from the Island. Most staff members were allowed to visit the Island only on their days off, but since everybody knew Dan, he could jump on the boat and spend a few hours there in the evening without consequence. So Dan decided to check out what all the fun was about.

The new phenomenon was a type of bodyboard surfing. It was most likely the first extreme sport on the Island. It involved running on the beach, jumping into the water, and riding over the water on small boards, regardless of whether there were waves or not. It was like skipping rocks, but with people! The aim was to see who could surf the longest.

When Dan returned with his report, he convinced me I had to see it. As we headed to the Island one afternoon after work, Dan continued raving about this unique sport's intensity and excitement. When we arrived, I saw how much everyone enjoyed it — both staff and campers — and kept trying to see how far they could skim on the water. Dan's fellow buddies who had grown up in the area were the bravest of these, always trying to show off that they were professionals at everything related to Word of Life and Schroon Lake.

Eventually, Dan stood up and walked to the front of the crowd near the water's edge.

"I'll take that bodyboard if you're done with it." He told one of the guys that had just gotten out of the water.

"Good luck, kid. Try not to hurt yourself." Dan grabbed the board and backed up to get a running start. As more people saw him attempting the challenge, they cheered him on. As a staff kid, he was well-known. The cheers were loud, bolstering his confidence and excitement. He ran forward with the board held to his chest and flew into the air, ready to hit the water. And hit the water he did. He didn't "skim" the surface at all, but rather, he plunged right in with a dismal "plop." Yet, for Dan, this was a success! He was always like that: confronting a new challenge without fear, finding satisfaction. So, when God called him to go to Hungary, he faced the task with courage — not with bravado, as in extreme sports, but with realistic motivation to do something for God.

Chef Jim Dise put me into my place - picture taken by Dan.

Early Dating Attempts

However, for Dan, dating was a challenge he approached with some hesitation. At the end of the summer, there was a banquet where it was expected to ask a girl to go with you. Dan and I were clueless about girls, so asking one to the banquet seemed intimidating. Talking about whom we would like to go with seemed much easier, so that summer, there was a lot of talk without much action.

My dating standards at the time had been heavily influenced by my roommate, Carl. Some viewed him as legalistic, but he was a young man of prayer and conviction, and I was determined to have

41

the same standards. In retrospect, however, I was placing importance on all the wrong things. Carl used Deuteronomy 22:5 to convince others that women should only wear skirts and dresses, not pants. He reasoned that pants were men's clothing. He heavily promoted this principle that summer, and his ideas made sense to me as a young'un.

Of course, we were both passionate about pleasing God, but in our young faith, we needed wisdom. Quickly, I was persuaded by the verse out of context, which framed my thinking. It's embarrassing now, but at the time, I felt that I was standing up for what was right. There must have been something in my heart that made me realize I was wrong, though, because when Dan asked me who I would take to the banquet, I didn't want to tell him who she was.

"C'mon, Butler," Dan prodded. "You got to tell me who you're thinking of taking." I glanced at him nervously, knowing he would reprimand me for my choice since the only thing I knew about her was that she only wore skirts and dresses. "At least give me a hint" Dan urged, looking at me expectantly.

"Ok, fine… Her initials are SB," I replied reluctantly.

"SB, huh?" Dan paused, thinking, "Butler, of all the girls you talk to, none of them has those initials, unless I forgot someone."

"Well," I started, "I haven't talked to her much." Dan looked at me quizzically.

"Then why do you want to take her to the banquet?" Dan asked, already frowning at the hint of where the conversation was headed.

"In Deuteronomy 22, it says women shouldn't wear men's clothes…" Dan rolled his eyes as the words left my mouth, but I continued, "I think it's important, Dan. You should, too."

"I don't think that's right. You should stay away from that kind of thinking." Dan looked at me seriously, "Maybe this SB girl only wears skirts and dresses, but what about the rest of her personality? You don't know anything about her."

"Well, I'll get to know her," I said confidently.

"I'm serious, Butler. Pretty much all the girls I know wear pants, and they are great. My mom wears pants and is a godly woman."

" 'Therefore, all who are mature, let's have this attitude; and if in anything you have a different attitude, God will reveal that to you as well.' Philippians 3:15," I quoted. "I'll be patient with you since you have different standards, but I hope you will see the truth one day." Dan shook his head at me, chuckling.

Luckily, my legalistic views of dating did not last long past that summer. I was thankful to have a friend who didn't mind opposing me where I was wrong. I now realize this standard was absurd and only a personal preference. Every culture is different, and what is suitable and modest in each culture varies. God calls us to present our bodies as a living sacrifice and to honor Him in all that we do. Honoring God through our dress can take different forms for different people.

Later, when I went overseas, this concept became very important. Ironically, it would be considered immodest in Central Asia if a woman did not wear pants under her dress. In that context, all our Western legalistic *preferences* became immodest.

While Dan opposed me on my legalistic standards, I would tease him about his preferences. He always seemed to want a girl from a Christian family. "Well, what am I? I didn't come from a Christian family. Does that make me worse? Should no Christian girl date me?" Our idiosyncrasies often encouraged each other until we became more convinced of specific ideas, justifying them with excuses.

That summer, he was still establishing his standards but was considering asking Jodi Lough. Jodi was the daughter of the Word of Life Inn director, so Dan had practically grown up with her. Dan wanted to be with someone he felt comfortable with, and Jodi was like a sister to him.

But before Dan decided to ask her, he started to urge me to ask her. He did this based on a single event that occurred a few weeks prior to the banquet. We both took the boat to the Island to join the Teens Involved event. Afterward, I ended up on the boat with the Lough family as we headed towards the Inn. The Loughs and I had a pleasant conversation, and then, as we were getting up to leave, Mr. Lough inquired, "As a participant of Teens Involved, could you join us for ice cream?" I eagerly nodded since I greatly respected the Lough family and knew their son, Don, who worked in the bakery during the summer of 1981.

So, we, including their daughter, Jodi, had a pleasant time getting ice cream as Mr. and Mrs. Lough shared their love story, which connected to where I was from. They mentioned how they met at the Bible Memory Association Camp in Perth, NY, and later, their first date was at the WOL Inn. I didn't think much of this event until I mentioned it to Dan the next day.

Dan looked at me, utterly shocked, "They invited you for ice cream?!" He quickly continued with a slew of questions, "Was anyone else there? Or was it just you? Did they talk to you about anything special?"

"It was just me. It was a nice time. They just shared their love story, and other than that, the conversation was mainly about Teens Involved."[13] I shrugged, but Dan stared at me with his eyes wide.

"They shared their *love* story?!" Bubar exclaimed, "Butler, c'mon. They are trying to set you up with Jodi. They are open to you taking her to the banquet!" I waved away his comments, thinking them absurd. Jodi was a year or so younger than us, and I doubted that a respectable family like the Loughs would try to set up their 14-year-old daughter with me.

"Well, how did they go about inviting you?" Dan interrogated.

"Bubar, the only thing that happened was that Mr. Lough came up to me and said, 'As a participant of Teens Involved, could you join us for ice cream?' " I barely got out the rest of the question before Dan responded.

"*As a participant of Teens Involved*? No way. That is not the reason they invited you. We're all participants, but I don't see them inviting anyone else to ice cream!" I laughed and continued to ignore him, but he persisted in discussing all the possibilities and how crazy the situation was. Then he sputtered out, "You should ask her to the banquet! That's what her parents want. You respect them so much, so you should do what they want. I'm serious." Dan looked at me excitedly.

"I don't even know her that well, Dan," I responded, exasperated.

"Ha," Dan scoffed. "That didn't seem to be an issue with the SB girl. 'I'll just get to know her'?" Looking smug, knowing he had caught me red-handed.

"They weren't trying to set me up, Dan," I said with finality, trying to shut down the conversation so I wouldn't have to give my real reason.

My "standards" had overtaken my thinking. However, Dan could not get over what happened... *As a participant of Teens Involved...as a participant of Teens Involved...* this became Dan's mantra. He kept on reading into the situation and saying these words. This talk dominated the day and tended to go overboard. Perhaps Mr. Lough heard him talking, through the window, because he appeared in the bakery shortly after. He came in as pleasant as always and greeted us. After he left, Dan continued the banter, and

Mr. Lough walked in again, surprising us. After a third visit, we tended to lower our voices, realizing others could hear our conversations.

It should have stopped us from talking about it altogether, but Dan loved to share his perspective at my expense for years. After a week of Dan teasing me and urging me to ask Jodi, he finally decided to ask her himself. I asked my intended date, too, and she said yes. He was not underhanded in any way, but all this talk about Jodi gave him the confidence to ask her himself. He knew that, as another participant in Teens Involved, his chances were high.

Jodi's father, Mr. Lough, had made a rule that any guy wanting to ask his daughter out had to ask for his permission first. Jodi knew that the banquet was coming up soon and that any guy could ask her, so she reminded her father of their rule. She hoped that her father would say "no" to any of the guys she didn't want to go out with. (By the way, I have her permission to share this.)

So, when Dan approached Jodi to ask her to the banquet, Jodi immediately said, "Well, Dan, I don't know if I can. My dad's rule is that anyone who asks me out must get his permission first." Dan listened intently, nodding his head.

"Ok, I will ask him then," Dan said matter-of-factly with all the seriousness in the world. Jodi smiled at him politely. In reality, Jodi had her dad as a buffer because she did *not* want to go with Dan. This would be her first date, and she didn't want to waste it on someone who was like a brother to her. They'd even grown up calling each other's parents Aunt and Uncle. For Dan, that familiarity was perfect, but for her, that was what could ruin it all. Jodi prepared to talk to her father as soon as she got home and to warn him to say no to Dan.

But Dan ultimately intercepted Jodi's well-crafted plans because he immediately left to find her dad. "Hey, Uncle Don, I have a very important question to ask you."

Mr. Lough smiled, "Well, what is it, Danny?"

"I would like to take Jodi to the STC banquet." Dan wrung his hands together as he waited for Mr. Lough's response.

"Thank you for asking me," Mr. Lough started. "First, I want to tell you why I want you to ask me first." Dan listened intently, and Mr. Lough continued to speak about honoring Jodi and valuing her. Throughout Mr. Lough's hefty monologue, Dan nodded and listened, fully absorbed. When Mr. Lough finished, Dan stared at him in awe.

"Wow, Uncle Don," Dan stood there shaking his head in amazement, "that is *really* great. I will do the same thing if I ever have a daughter!" Mr. Lough chuckled at Dan's enthusiasm and proceeded to give him permission to take Jodi to the banquet. "I will do my best to make you proud, Uncle Don." Dan firmly shook Mr. Lough's hand and left the conversation feeling encouraged.

Later that day, Jodi got home, ready to warn her dad of Dan's upcoming question. But before she could inform him, he happily told her that he had given Dan his permission. Jodi's mouth dropped as she stared at her father in shock.

"Dad!" she screamed, tears brimming in her eyes. I did not want to go with Danny Bubar! He's like a brother!" Her father looked at her, shocked by her reaction.

Mr. Lough felt compassion for his daughter, but he knew she had to honor the decision. "Well, I'm sorry, Jodi, but you didn't tell me that," Mr. Lough sighed, "and I gave him permission, so you have to honor that and go with him. He is a great young man, and I know he will treat you well at the banquet." Jodi groaned in frustration at her predicament, mourning the loss of a romantic first date.[14]

At the banquet, Dan was kind to Jodi the whole night, despite her inattentiveness towards him. Meanwhile, I sat awkwardly at a table with SB, not initiating much conversation. I realized that I had not been honoring her like Dan was honoring Jodi because I only asked her. After all, she didn't wear "men's clothes." Because of this, I didn't have the heart to get to know her, and we both ended up having a pretty dull night with little interaction between us. As I sat at the table looking at my other friends and their booming conversation with their dates, I realized that maybe my standards weren't so great.

Connecting to WOL Staff

Dan always tried to imply that I was one of those kids with a WOL connection. Now, a *staff brat* was the term we gave to those kids whose parents worked for WOL. Many of us typical kids felt that these kids had extra privileges; of course, being the friend of a WOL'er had its benefits, but I still wasn't connected. Dan found an amusing loophole, though. During the summers of 1981 and 1982, our summer paychecks were signed by M. A. Butler, who had no relation to me whatsoever. But occasionally, someone would ask if I was related to the person whose signature adorned our bi-weekly checks. I would deny it and brush it off.

However, Bubar enjoyed teasing me by telling others, "Don't you know his father signs your check?" He even went as far as joking that any mistreatment towards me could result in a loss of a paycheck. Later that summer, when Dan's parents were set to meet up with M. A. Butler for a meal, they invited me along. I wasn't too keen on the idea as I didn't want the rumors about me being his son to spiral out of control, so I never met the man responsible for my honorary "staff brat" title.

The summer of 1982 stands out vividly as a transformative period for Dan and me. Our laughter and camaraderie faced a challenge with the summer ending Bible Institute graduation. This event required us to significantly increase our work production, as we were tasked with preparing enough desserts and bread for three times our typical summer clientele. When we parted ways, our summer laid the foundation for our incredible friendship.

1982 Inn STC, Bubar back right with hat, next to Eric. I am sitting next to Paul Dilger (in white), my sister over his other shoulder

Chapter Four

Our High School Comradery

In our spiritual lives, teenagers often approach our WOL club assignments and duties on autopilot. However, even though I genuinely wanted to serve the Lord, there were times when I struggled with maintaining a clear vision and sincerity in moving forward. Despite this, my experience in public school kept me spiritually alert. Our school situations differed since I attended a public school while Dan was in a Christian school. One day, I sat in the hallway waiting for homeroom to start, and a classmate approached me.

"Did you do your math homework?" she asked.

I said, "Yes, I did, why?"

She immediately brightened up with hope. "Let me see it," as if insisting happily would make it more palatable. She had no issue with what she was asking.

I stared at her blankly, surprised by her request and fumbling about how to respond to her well. My brain scurried with the possibility that she wasn't asking to cheat. But I knew the truth as I looked at her insistent, outstretched hand.

"Well, I am not going to show it to you," I replied. She looked hurt and offended.

"What? Why not?" Her startled, crestfallen face kept me from blurting out what I thought was obvious: *Cheating is wrong*! My hands started to sweat, and I prayed for the right thing to say.

"Well," I started tentatively, "I believe everyone should do their own work…" I paused as I thought of my memory verse from WOL, Galatians 6:4, *"But let every man prove his own work, and then shall he have rejoicing in himself alone, and not in another."* The girl raised an eyebrow at me and scoffed, "So you won't show it to me?" All the previous sadness on her face gave way to disgust and frustration as she stomped away to join a different classmate.

I felt relieved when she walked out of sight, knowing I had done the right thing, even if it was hard. I thanked God for bringing that verse to mind and was thankful I had memorized it during my time in the Word of Life Club. She likely did not understand what I was saying, but I felt a renewed confidence that God would give wisdom to interact with unbelievers and that he would work in their hearts.

After the summertime, Bubar and I both had to face the school year. While we worked during the summer, we received constant spiritual input and discipline; however, during the school year, we were challenged to apply what we had learned and discipline ourselves. Our school situations probably looked very different, but we each faced our own challenges.

I recall starting my summer at the Inn in 1982 when Paul Bubar spoke to the newly arrived staff, saying, "A servant is a person who never stops obeying." For both of us, obedience became a daily challenge, especially in public school.

Friendly Rivalry

During the school year, Dan and I would occasionally see each other. I saw Dan during the winter; our church already had a friendly rivalry with Dan's church because of our school basketball teams. Although I was not a part of Perth Bible's school, I attended the Mountainside vs. Perth basketball games. This event always amused me since Tim, who had invited me to church, was the star on the Perth team, and Dan played on the other.

After the game, Dan said, "Hey, Butler, good game. Too bad your team lost this time." Then he changed the subject, "Great to see you. Will you be at Snow Camp?"

"Yes, and I look forward to it." The crowd interrupted our chat, but the small connection always meant something to us both.

The rivalry was intense enough that whenever I chatted with some of the "Mountainsiders" after the game, the "Perthites" would jokingly shame me and ask, "Why are you talking to them? Where is your team spirit?"

This rivalry continued during snow camps, as all the regional churches attended the same weekend. Again, there was often significant competition between his church and ours. In between the banter, we chatted at times.

Club and Quiz Team

My highlight of the school week was attending the church's Word of Life Club, which provided fellowship and encouragement. The youth group had weekly lessons, verses to memorize, and a quiet time booklet to fill out. Of course, there wasn't any punishment for not doing these things, but I strived to be consistent in them all. In looking back, the club's purpose was to prepare for ministry in one's church—at least that is what it seemed like.

Additionally, this program prepared youth to attend the Bible Institute (BI) later since many of the disciplines were the same. I enjoyed the challenge of passing the Bible Memory exams to get scholarships for the BI. At first, I had no idea what this meant, but these scholarships immensely helped pay for my first year of study.

Part of Word of Life Clubs was the Spring "Teens Involved," where area churches gathered for participation, including Perth Bible and Dan's church Mountainside Bible Chapel. This was a rare opportunity to see Dan during the school year. The time included competition-like events in multiple areas, allowing us to practice our God-given skills. There was preaching, singing, and other ministries, such as puppeteering. Each event allowed us to get to know fellow believers our age and receive helpful feedback from those who judged the activity.

Ultimately, the event's high point was the quiz team, at least for Dan and me. The quiz team was a healthy competition where teens were quizzed on verses and other club lesson material. So naturally, the teens who consistently completed all the club requirements and attended had the advantage.

I always worked hard to study all the material, seeing it as an opportunity to better prepare for ministry. Additionally, it was exciting when my church's team, Perth Bible, won. Despite our efforts, we often felt overshadowed by Dan Bubar's team at Mountainside Bible Chapel. Dan was constantly soaked in the quiz material as a Word of Life staff kid. Also, he was hard-working, studious, and zealous.

With this history of rivalry, the Perth team strongly desired to defeat Mountainside in the quiz competition. Our team was newer, so we struggled with the depth of the competition. Mountainside had years of experience, plus proximity to Word of Life. They were the true Word of Life church and excelled in everything related to the organization. They were intimidating. The only times we felt like we had a fighting chance were when Dan reached the quota for answering questions and had to sit down, but even then, we usually lost.

But in our second season, our team was determined to win. We dedicated ourselves to studying together. One time, we did so over lasagna, which was a terrible idea because it left all of us lethargic with little mental energy. However, despite this, the bonding experience prepared us as a team for competition.

Meanwhile, Mountainside was also diligently setting aside time for serious study sessions, probably without carb-induced lethargy. Dan wrote me a letter to pre-warn me, saying: *"We are having a quiz team breakfast at the Loughs' tomorrow morning in a last attempt to get our team together before our area competition. Last Sunday night, we had a teen night in our church, and I know that some people are going to win at nationals, especially in the vocal area (duets, solos). Well, maybe I am a bit prejudiced, but not much."*

Finally, the day arrived when we were competing again at the regional Teens Involved event. Both teams were on the edge of their seats, ready for the competition to begin, anticipating victory. The speaker asked the first question, and immediately, I knew the answer and sprang out of my seat. But, to my dismay, I realized I was the third to stand after two teens from Mountainside. Of course, the first was Dan, who answered the question confidently and correctly, scoring 1-0. It didn't feel like a great way to start, but we pushed on.

Question number two came and went with Dan showing off his speed and smarts. By question three, I knew I had to be faster with my standing, so I practically jumped out of my seat before the speaker finished the question. And finally, my team was on the scoreboard as I gave the correct answer.

Bubar stole the show, and his following answer came faster than we could even process the question. Then he dominated the following two questions as well, but now he had to sit down because he had reached his quota. Now, it was our chance to come back. Our whole strategy was to wait for Dan to *quiz out*!

Eventually, I answered enough questions to join Dan in quizzing out. We sat cheering for our respective teams, and I clapped louder when our team was only a point behind; maybe we could do this and beat Mountainside. But their quiz team didn't relent; they blasted through the last of the questions, getting many more right than our team. We were way behind, but we felt the loss strongly since we had worked so hard to win.

Dan exemplified one of the memory verses: "If a man also strives for masteries, yet is he not crowned, except he strives *lawfully*" (2 Tim. 2:5). In other words, he mastered the competition correctly and was rewarded. He strived to master the WOL lesson booklet used for the quizzing sessions. He knew the lessons and verses by heart. He was quick to his feet, and his answers were correct. I will fully admit that I could not go toe-to-toe with him on quizzing, but I could follow his example in quizzing out.

Tragedy and a Call to Missions

Sitting in my school class in the spring of 1983, I was called out, "Please go to the principal's office." Unaware of why, I was perplexed about what was happening.

As I entered the office, my youth pastor stood there—unexpectedly. "I just talked to your sister, and I am sorry to tell you this, but your friend Michele has died."

"What? How did it happen?"

At that point, a massive blur enveloped my mind. Pastor Geremia asked, "Would you like to head home? I will be taking Janet back. She went to retrieve her belongings." I thought it was better to continue the day and not think about it.

Michele, my sister's best friend, was murdered by her stepfather.[15] It was a tragic event that left those who knew her in shock. She was so young and a person who hung with us at church and in our home.

When I came home from school, I approached my sister's room and asked if she was all right. My question only made her more aware, and she started to cry again. As a teenager, unprepared to comfort my sister, I walked away.

Death was not familiar to me, nor was how to comfort another or even handle my own grief. I recalled my grandpa's funeral a year and a half before, but I was ill-prepared to face the death of a friend. It affected my sister and me greatly.

Mission Challenge Starts with Prayer

When Dan and I worked in the Burning Bakery the previous summer, my sister had recruited three friends to join her. Two joined her in Food Prep, but her best friend, Michele, wanted to work as a waitress.

It is incredible to think about that summer, as we both lived through it with our best friends.

Michele had a heart for serving others and loved being around people, making her work very fulfilling.

Her dedication to God grew a lot that summer. She committed her life to serving God wherever he wanted her to go, and she was especially moved by one of the summer presenters, Howie Williams.

Howie desired to influence others for the Lord and raise awareness about the least-reached areas worldwide, particularly among Turks. No other missionary I knew did what he did. He handed out country cards for prayer for least-reached areas, expecting God to work. He also recruited people to become pen pals with Turks and encouraged them to pray for them.

I asked him why he did this. He responded, "My purpose in handing out cards with reference to Turkey was to raise interest in the spiritual needs of Turks and to recruit fellow journeyers to join us in ministry among Turks."[16] Howie served on staff in Schroon Lake for three years, from 1977 to 1979, sensing a call to reach Turks with the gospel. As a single man, he surveyed the country of Turkey and visited Iran before the 1979 revolution. His step of faith is remembered on the WOLBI campus with a dorm called *Turkey*.

He said, "My calling was to the Turks. I began praying for Turkey in the summer of '68 after learning that, at that time, there were about 100 believers who had come from the majority religion. The country's population was about 44 million [in 1979]." Imagine only 100 believers out of 44 million? Today, 40 years later, there are still only 10-15,000 Turkish believers with a population of 82 million. The need is still overwhelming.

Despite Howie's singleness and the lack of churches to partner with in that land, he went there to learn the language and form relationships with Muslims. During his summer visit to the Inn in 1982, he distributed Operation World-affiliated prayer cards for the least-reached countries. After he spoke, he asked individuals to come forward, take a country card, and commit to praying for this country to encourage prayer and awareness of these least-reached lands.

That day, Michele and I, along with many others, went forward to receive a country card. She lined up before me and received one for Bangladesh; I got one for Turkey.

When I saw her card, I said, "Oh, Bangladesh. I read a good book about that country." She responded, "Do you want to switch? I'm interested in your card because I have a pen pal there." So, we switched cards.

After this, she mentioned how she wanted to visit Turkey. I heard another missionary say that a calling to serve in another country is usually related to how far our prayers will go. We will only go if we are willing to pray about distant places. Since she was praying for this country, she felt a movement in her heart to go there someday.

The prayer card that Howie Williams handed out - After praying, I visited Bangladesh in 1986.

However, during her teenage years, her mission field, much like mine, was at school. She attended the public school in Amsterdam, NY, while my sister and I attended about 10 miles up the road in Fonda. She, too, strived to live for the Lord in this environment. Life in public school was difficult, but she invited some of her friends to the WOL all-nighter at our church that year. Together, we went bowling, attempting to show that Christians can have fun.

Are you willing to go?

At the funeral, Pastor Geremia spoke on serving God with your life, just like Michele had. Our youth pastor said, "What is your life? It appears as a (water) vapor and then vanishes away."

"What will you do with your life? Life is short. Will you live for the Lord as Michele wanted to but did not have the chance? Perhaps some of you will desire to serve overseas, just as she had hoped to do one day." These words touched my heart, and I realized the brevity of life. What did the Lord want with my life?

At the same time, I was in shock and at a loss for words to comfort those around me. I sat in sorrow alongside my sister and others as the pastor's words rang in my head. As a pallbearer of her casket, I wanted to have the same heart for ministry as Michele had, but at that moment, I felt a deep need for comfort.

At the funeral, I gave my sister the needed hug, which was long overdue. Another of the pallbearers was my roommate from that

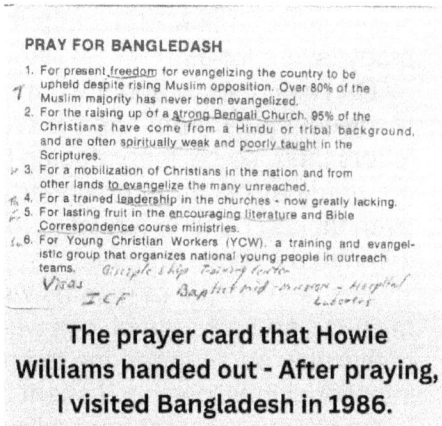

summer. He took Michele to the STC banquet, so the loss had many layers for us.

Dan didn't know about what had happened to Michele, but I received a letter from him the day after her death. He rarely sent me letters then, so his letter couldn't have come at a better time. I read his words as he wrote about the random goings-on in his life, and even though none of it related to what I was going through, I was comforted to hear from him.

The next couple of months went by with sadness hanging over my head and a sense of loss whenever I looked at my sister, yet all of this only encouraged me to press more into God and be more intentional in fellowship. I spent time with other Christians, soaking in the encouragement from fellowshipping with others at church, especially the weekend students from Word of Life.

I joined them in the bus ministry, knocking on doors and inviting kids to church. It gave me perspective as I remembered others and their need for Christ. With my newfound awareness of the brevity of life, I wanted to use mine wholeheartedly for God, and I saw an urgency in sharing the gospel with others, realizing that we never know when life can end.

Spring Bible Conference

A few weeks later, I was about to go to the Word of Life Spring Bible Conference. I was excited for this time of spiritual growth and fellowship, and I knew I would see some of my Word of Life friends like Dan. As I packed to head to the conference, my mom approached me with a grim look on her face. Her lips were tight, and I looked at her, asking, "What's wrong?"

"Your Dad came home last night, and he packed his clothes. He's not coming back." She said this stoically, and I nodded back in the same manner, even though my insides were tumbling over one other.

I quickly packed the rest of my things as my mind raced. I'd known my parents were having troubles, and there were plenty of times when I had no idea where my dad was, but for him to not come back? I didn't believe it. I didn't understand what his leaving meant, and like any child, I hoped that my parents would get back together.

On the drive to Word of Life, I prayed and trusted God. I knew that even at this low point, God was with me, and he had a plan. I could trust his plan, and he would continue to lead and provide.

Amidst my sorrow, I felt hopeful about a weekend away to focus on God and what He had in store for me.

Dan and I were ecstatic to see each other. Since he worked at the Inn, he had to miss some of the sessions, but whenever he was there, we sat together, intently taking notes. I didn't mention my parents' separation to anyone that weekend. I just wanted to set my mind on learning from the messages. One of the speakers was Georgi Vins, a Russian minister who the communist government had imprisoned for his ministry. He praised God that he was released in a prisoner exchange by President Carter but sought for the Western church to pray for the persecuted church that remained in the USSR.[17]

Dan and I were amazed by his dedication to ministry and his selflessness for God. During a break near the lake, Dan said, "What do you think about him? His commitment astonishes me." I said, "Yeah, to go through that in a communist environment is unbelievable. What did you think about his proposal when he asked his wife-to-be, 'Are you prepared to follow me to prison — if so, marry me?'"

Dan mused, "Maybe we should try that method here in the US? Even though he faced much opposition, he still boldly proclaimed the word of the Lord. I stand amazed."[18]

As we reflected on our privileged lives, another speaker challenged us to venture into the mission field.

I was thrilled to hear Dr. Stephen Olford again, who spoke in 1982 at the Inn. His British accent and quick wit focused our attention. He alluded to his upbringing as a missionary kid and the importance of the Word. He rolled his Rs to a resounding conviction for the Word of God when possible. He ministered in New York City during the 1980s and was a well-known expositor and preacher.

Dr. Olford's message focused on *Preaching the Word*, and his sessions sprinkled in a strong missionary focus. Right before his last session, Dan and I again talked, this time near the lake, pondering what God had in store for us. We both felt a deep stirring to serve God fully, regardless of the consequences. We wanted to preach the gospel to those who were lost. The call rang out for those who will obey this calling to preach the Word. Dr. Olford said, "Come, commit, and pray at the front." I stepped out, and on the left side of the Council Hall stage, I kneeled and prayed, committing my life to the Lord to do his will. From that day, preaching the Word became a focus for both of us. The call to do God's will took hold in my heart from then on, aligning it with his purposes.[19] For Dan, he wanted to preach the Word to the world's youth.

Summer of 1983 - Dan's Escape

The summer of 1983 found Dan in the bakery on the Island and I at the Inn. In the letter that arrived at the time of Michele's death, Dan stated that Mike Bush had instructed him to write to me. He wrote, *"Don Lough [Jr] is going to work at the Inn [Garden Café[20]], and [he] would like it if I worked there w/him. I have decided upon the Island because I would be baking for 400 instead of 200 and would provide more better practical experience [sic]. Right now (Feb 1983), I am working at the Inn like crazy."[21]* Jokingly, Dan ended the letter with, *"Come to the Island even though Jodi Lough is working at the Inn."*

Dan loved the Island and, as soon as possible, found a place to serve there. Whenever he was in NY for the summer, during university, this was where he served and spent his time.

That summer, I worked instead with "Robin the Baker," who married chef Dave Johnson. She was a professional baker and gifted at decorating cakes.

On days off or half days off, Dan and I met up. I went to the Island for a few hours, or he came to town, crashing at grandma Swanson's house. There, he did his laundry and ate lunch or whatever goodies his grandma had for us.

I would pop in for an hour or so in the late afternoon since this was a short walk from the Inn property. I wanted to catch up with the latest happenings in our bakery world. I recall his grandma's gracious and kind manner. She was a genuinely kind lady and always encouraged us young boys. She had a great smile, and her eyes twinkled when she talked. She radiated wisdom in her speech, encouraging us to make wise choices.

One of the reasons he went to the Island was to "escape" the tension between him and any head chef at the Inn. At least, this was how he described it to others in the WOL circle years later. He summarized the Inn work of 1982 with statements of burned dinner rolls and the chef throwing pots and pans at him. Of course, this never happened. These embellished stories grew over time for dramatic effect. He likely wanted a change of scenery after working at the Inn all school year. But Dan's happy place was in the middle of Schroon Lake, not on its shores.

Island Drama

Dan spent his childhood summers on the Island because his dad was the program director and eventually became the director there. In 1958, Mr. Bubar was known for driving a motorcycle onto the stage to grab the campers' attention. He dressed up as a hippy and did his center-stage ride during Jack Wyrtzen's announcements, all planned, of course.

I remember this story because it was out of the ordinary, yet it was far from isolated. Paul Bubar's playful rogueries shaped Dan's sense of adventure and creativity. He loved his father and wanted to emulate him.

Another story Dan told me was that one evening after the lights went out, his dad called all the teens into the main meeting room. With all seriousness, Paul announced that one of the local prisons had experienced a jailbreak, and some prisoners had escaped into the Adirondacks. As he shared the details, someone came in and gave him a note. He read it and looked up gravely. An empty boat was found docked at the Island's northern end.

At this point, all the campers were seized with fear. You may be wondering, as I am now, *What was Mr. Bubar thinking?* I don't know, but Dan made it sound hilarious, and as a kid, I loved hearing about the latest shenanigans on the Island.

Dan went on to explain that, just after his dad described the prisoners' clothing, a man dressed like a prisoner walked by the door. Now, if you have been in the WOL Island tabernacle for meetings, screen doors on each lower side enable one to see outside.

Someone yelled, "Look, there's a guy outside that door!" This event furthered the evening drama. Most likely, the whole thing was revealed as a hoax, and the campers returned to their cabins with a great story, but Dan was never interested in those extra details. He enjoyed relaying the hysteria of it all.

These techniques are no longer used today, for obvious reasons, though I am sure Dan's "Bubar embellishment" was applied to what he told me; however, it made a great story for two teenagers. I share it here because it illustrates how Dan discussed his dad. His dad was creative and not afraid to try unconventional ideas. He loved kids and Jesus, and anything that would bring them together.

The culture and national perspective on scare tactics have changed, and I shudder to think of some of the events —

questionable today — that we all participated in at some point. But Dan and I came from that period, and it was, frankly, a time that allowed for creative and crazy fun.

In Bubar's mind, every story was embellished and grew over time, so even now, one cannot be sure what actually took place with all the exaggerations. However, I know we enjoyed retelling these adventures.

Lessons to Learn

We participated in the preaching competition each year during the springtime for Teens Involved. Usually, we preached only to the judges or those who happened to step into the room, so Dan and I had no chance to evaluate each other. The practice helped us preach the Word in a safe context, and the evaluations prepared us for our future situations. I don't remember either of us winning anything, but it certainly prepared us well.

During the summer, we had the opportunity to discuss our messages for Teens Involved.

"What did you preach on, Bubar?" I continued, "I have chosen to preach on Hebrews 3:13, where we need not to harden our hearts but to listen today to the Lord's voice."

"I am speaking about prayer," Dan responded. "I read R.A. Torrey's book, *How to Pray*. So I am talking about that."

In my cheekiness, I responded, "Is this the Holy Spirit working in Torrey or you?"

"Well, that book meant a lot to me and challenged me," he said.

In my hypocrisy, my sermon the year before was on being a fisher of men when Jesus said, *Follow me.* This idea is heavily promoted in the book my uncle and aunt gave me for Christmas, *In His Steps,* by Charles M. Sheldon. I asked for an application, "What would Jesus do?" In this way, we do allow what we read to influence us.

This reminded me of Dan's dad jokingly saying, "Originality is forgetting where you got it from." We often misapplied this motto to most of our great ideas, taking credit where we shouldn't have, especially when we thought we had said something profound.

Despite our occasional hypocrisy, our teenage experiences helped us develop our responsibilities and relationships. The bakery had deadlines and expectations for preparing items for hundreds of people. Our interactions with others became like sandpaper smoothing rough edges. Every little action carved our character for the better. Of course, our selfishness hindered our growth, but we did aim to take daily steps toward faithfulness, dependability, and honesty.

Learning about Calling

As we share about our mission call, please bear with me as I lay some groundwork for what the summer training and staff program meant to Dan and me. Dan's whole experience was with the WOL family and year-round activities, but for me, it was mainly the summer programs and clubs. Hearing God's call on our lives was not a one-time decision. For us, "calling" meant knowing and doing God's will. We sensed the warning against hypocrisy in what Ken Dady said: "I can't hear you because your actions speak louder than your words."

The summer staff program provided us with an intense biblical foundation during our teenage years, benefiting and shaping our lives. We worked at WOL for at least seven summers — I at the Inn, and Dan mostly at the Island. Staff interactions led to spiritual conversations, and the meetings continually challenged our way of living. While going through all my papers at my mom's house after her death, I found notes from those WOL summers. Jack Wyrtzen spoke about reaching the lost, and David Wyrtzen talked about how to live wisely. Others, such as Ken Dady, Paul Bubar, and Sketch Erickson, all spoke directly to our teenage struggles. The summer staff training was a spiritual boot camp preparing us to serve.

From approximately 1983 to 1987, Ric Graham served as the staff director at the Inn. He was a former biker with an offbeat personality and wanted the staff to hear some of the best speakers. He invited some of the main speakers to address the staff in the old Swan Club's Icehouse, a quaint location for these evening times. The hard benches kept us awake, along with the night insects that sometimes narrowed their focus on one of the staffers. Our sapling hearts began to attach their roots to the Word of God and fellowship.

Additionally, we attended the general meeting, which all guests at the Inn attended. As teenagers, we had no idea who these speakers were but learned to love them.

Learning to Love the Word

Some speakers blew Dan and me away, and we'd talk excitedly about how they motivated us. On Wednesday night, Don Lough, Sr. introduced a quirky professor with dark-framed glasses and a bow tie. His name was Dr. Howard Hendricks. It was not a name I knew, and I thought, "This man is going to bore us," but I soon learned how wrong I was.

I took meticulous notes and could not believe the insights he provided during his hour-long talk. As I neared the end of my paper, my writing became smaller, trying to fit in his wise words. His challenge to think more deeply about the Word of God sparked a deeper interest in my heart.

Years later, this man's influence became even more meaningful when I attended Dallas Theological Seminary and took a few of his classes. Later, his publication, *Living by the Book,* became my standard text for teaching new believers how to study the Bible.

One speaker discussed Jesus in the Garden of Gethsemane, saying, "Could you not spend one hour with me?" The speaker challenged us to spend an hour a day with the Lord. "It is not just a quiet time but a time of unhurried meditation and prayer without a defined structure." I decided to take time after work to try this. A hollowed-out hillside hosted summer concerts each Tuesday evening, and the area sloped downward toward the Inn's backyard pond, with a small island serving as the stage. It provided the perfect spot—multiple layers of trees with the Adirondack Mountains as the backdrop —a beautiful place to meditate.

These times of reflection helped me think about life, witnessing, and the choices I needed to make. I am sure Dan heard similar challenges while he worked on the Island.

Pepto-Bismol Generation

One night, an 81-year-old man was called up, and his appearance was not promising. Any staff teenager could have wondered why we should listen to this man who could barely move. He said in a slow southern drawl, "I'm not part of the Pepsi generation but part of the Pepto-Bismol generation." We all laughed, and he had our full attention.

The preacher was Vance Havner (1901-1986). At that point, I did not know what a privilege it was to hear this man. He was a favorite among the summer speakers, and I am grateful that during the summers of 1981 to 1983, staff were required to attend some of the evening programs.[22]

He asked, 'Have you missed your miracle? He said that he surveyed multiple congregations and asked the same question. *Do you believe that you have missed God's blessing in your life?* Surprisingly, based on his testimony, over 50% of the audience raised their hands. They believed they'd missed God's miracle or blessing in their lives. He preached about the importance of complete obedience to the Lord to experience God's miracles and blessings firsthand. I committed to the Lord not to miss his miracle and to live free from the regrets disobedience brings.[23] That lesson still rings in my heart. The sessions, which took place at both the Inn and the Island, were a spiritual buffet, and these men of God understood how to deliver its delicacies in a witty manner. Their faithful lives exemplified perseverance in their devotion to God despite the bumps in the road.

The Bible Conference format is long gone, but these speakers gave Dan and me a love for hearing the Word of God preached and taught.

Finances: a Matter of Faith

My struggles with money were a common theme. At the end of the summer of 1984, a Bible Institute student stretched my faith by asking me to accompany him on a short-term trip.

Charlie Ebron was on my bus route at Perth Bible, where he did his BI ministry hours on weekends. Now Charlie, who was from Newark, NJ, was a big guy and had even tried out as a lineman for the New York Jets. At 6'8", he occupied a whole seat on the bus, yet he was as gentle as a teddy bear with the kids. And he was passionate about evangelism. That summer, when we were both working at WOL Inn, he had the crazy idea that we should take a "missions trip" during the two free weeks before my first year and his second year.

He planned to visit Toronto, New York City, and the City Mission in Atlantic City. I'd been planning to make some real money then, but he suggested we spend it instead. At first, I was not convinced. *Where will we get all the money?*

I got to know.

Charlie would say, "My Father owns the cattle on a thousand hills, so I am sure he could give us one."

63

I let Dan know I'd be going and that I'd be a day late for orientation, so he should save me a lower bunk. Reluctantly, Dan said he would see what he could do.

Sure enough, the Lord provided the necessary funds and accommodations. In Toronto, we stayed with an open-air evangelist; for NYC, we stayed at Charlie's mom's place in Newark, and then with Rex Whitman at the Atlantic City Mission.

Charlie had me preach on the street near Rockefeller Center in NYC to prepare me for serving. One person came up to listen, but I naturally felt very self-conscious. (Also during this school year Dan went with Charlie and he did the open air board outside a gay bar in NYC.)

One of Charlie's public tactics was talking loudly with me about the "King." He would say, "Did you talk to the King today?" He'd pause to create tension and then share about King Jesus, who died on the cross. His courage and faith strengthened my faith for years to come.

1985 outreach with Charlie Ebron in Montreal.

When I arrived on campus, Dan said, "Butler, you don't know what you've done to me. I've been going to bat for you to protect your lower bunk." He was laughably annoyed.

"Really? That's great!" I was surprised he'd taken the responsibility so seriously, even though it'd caused him trouble.

He responded, "Well, I negotiated a deal. Our roommate said that since you didn't show up on time, you shouldn't get to have the lower bunk all year. So you have to switch each semester."

I considered this. "Not bad. Thanks." I was thankful for a friend who looked out for me in my absence. God had provided the finances for my trip and even, through Dan's maneuvering, a part-time bottom bunk!

Chapter Five - Rooming Through College

Earlier in the summer of 1984…

"Bubar, let's room together at the BI (Bible Institute)."

"Well, Butler, I already have a place in one of the big dorms."

"Can't we both put on our application that we want to room together?" wondering what the deal was.

"Yes, we can, but mine is already done." His response showed his foresight.

"Well, I'm requesting that you be my roommate, and we'll see where it goes."

After all, we ended up as roommates excited for the year and determined to study God's word diligently.

It was 1984, and my theme verse for the year was, "My soul is crushed with longing after your ordinances at all times" (Psalms 119:20, NASB 1995).

Whenever we could, we would get up early to pray together. I remember waking up in the bitter cold, a constant presence during New York winters. It would be dark outside and completely quiet, and Dan and I would shuffle into the hallway with weary eyes and chattering teeth. Yet we were both passionate about starting our day with prayer and encouraging each other in the pursuits each day held. We couldn't do it every week, nor all year, because of other commitments, but when we could, we tried to get together to pray.

We slowly tried to get others to join us, and eventually, we had three others who were willing to brave the early cold. We would each pray for God to guide and empower us to do his will that day. Although we didn't sit for long, that time together solidified our dependence on God for each day and taught us the importance of praying with colleagues, a practice we would continue in our future ministries.

I was thankful to have that time with Dan in the morning. It was a simple way to stay connected and be involved in each other's prayers and praises. We were so busy studying that finding time to refocus was good.

Dan was incredibly diligent in his studies. After the first two months, our good grades meant we weren't required to study at our desks during study hours. I took the opportunity to study with others, socialize, and engage in other activities with my time.

"Great, we're not confined to our desks. Do you wanna study together? Hang out in other places?" I anticipated.

Dan responded, "No way. My place is at my desk where I won't be distracted."

"Really, Bubar? What is the benefit of having this privilege if you're not going to use it?"

"He becomes poor that dealeth with a slack hand: but the hand of the diligent maketh rich," he responded.[24]

At first, I was a bit lost by his meaning, but then he looked me in the eye and added, "Butler, I will not be slack but will continue in diligence...at my desk."

He was intense in all his pursuits, always seeking to do the most that he could with the most efficiency. Later, he would show the same diligence in pre-field ministry, language study, and club ministry. Benefit and privilege did not motivate him as it did for typical young people. Nevertheless, I enjoyed my extra study freedom and made full use of the privilege.

Dan at his BI desk - class of 1985!

Physical Disciplines

Luckily, there was a built-in break during study hours. Dan would often use that time to play basketball and, on at least one occasion, to jog with me.

We both ran, but I had been on a high school cross-country team, which, although it won no titles, had competed well against other public school teams. In my final year, I usually placed third or fourth. I knew Dan hadn't been on a team.

So, when the BI announced the Turkey Trot — a three-mile race through campus — I felt I had some advantage. The course utilized the back trails near the maintenance building and featured minimal hills. I was overconfident. And Dan was ready to run his heart out.

The day arrived with bitterly cold weather, an Adirondack specialty. When the race started, we were running together.

"Butler, keep going. We can do this," he said. I just grunted. We were both huffing and puffing to keep up the pace, our egos charging our adrenaline. But I was getting cold and could feel a side ache coming on. I started to complain and said that I could not keep up.

"It is mind over matter. Do not listen to your body. Keep going." Dan tried to encourage me as any friend would, but he had the advantage.

"Bubar, go for it!" I mumbled.

With those words, he resumed his pace and was off. Cold air and frozen lips deflated my motivation. That night, I pondered and journaled how the race related to my Christian life; how I gave in to circumstances and was complacent about those who passed me.

Dan, on the other hand, had the strength to buffet his body and make it his servant. He'd placed in the top three. I was thankful to finish in a lowly ninth place, looking for somewhere warm as soon as possible.

He was persistent in practicing running, whereas I was not. I usually picked it up before the season or just before a race. But Dan, even before this, would run the highways after basketball practice and continue practicing. As a teenager, he prepared and won the Turkey Trot (Gallop)[25] in May 1982 in a few inches of snow. He was the only student of Mountainside to win this during his lifetime.

The following year, while in his second year at the BI, he said, *"I won't be winning the Gallop this year for I have been so busy & no time to run. However, I ran my fastest mile on the dirt [track] last week in 5:20"* (Fall 1985 letter). I thought, "Oh, yeah, Bubar, right! No time to run but doing a 5:20 mile! I could only dream of this." Dan was mentally tough and pushed himself based on an inner drive for improvement.

From New York to Tennessee

We were both swamped in our busy work at the Bible Institute and determined to make the most of our one year there. The year was a blur, yet it was challenging spiritually. We both grew in our walks with God, feeling more inclined towards ministry. At the year's end, Dan stayed on for the second-year program, the School of

Youth Ministry (SYME), to grow in ministry skills, and I headed off to Tennessee Temple University (TTU). Dan planned to join me eventually, but God led him to stay for the second year at WOL.

The first year there without Dan was tough. I was placed with a roommate I didn't know and who wasn't interested in getting to know me. A few Word of Life students were on campus, and I longed for Dan to arrive. I made some other friends, but finding comradery at University was difficult.

From the fall of 1985 to the summer of 1986, Dan and I exchanged letters to update each other on our latest learning and involvement. Dan was passionate about his involvement in various youth ministries. He wrote to me about a ministry where he witnessed 90 kids respond to the gospel message. It was exciting to read. He wanted to use all his time for God's glory and purposes.

With such a busy schedule during college, I found it easy to equate productivity with ministry. Many of us students quickly thought, "Well, I've done a lot already, so I've pleased God enough for today." It was easy to forget to focus on God rather than just my tasks. I realized that, while getting things done was great, I wanted to ensure that my heart was set on doing all unto God and not just for a sense of fulfillment.

I noticed that busyness easily distracted me from fellowshipping, so I made a conscious effort to find time to encourage others. In one of my mission classes, we discussed how the West tends to focus on time and tasks, whereas many other parts of the world prioritize relationships. An Iranian visionary, Sam Yeghnazar, is known for saying, "You have your fancy watches, but we, Iranians, have time." My wristwatch symbolized my issue; I lived based on what it said, making it more important than people. So, while at university, I decided to get rid of it. This small maneuver shaped me somewhat, but I was still driven to produce.

When summer arrived, I yearned to work at Word of Life with Dan, enjoying another summer together, but I felt the weight of bills. On the phone one day, I informed Dan that I still had Bible Institute tuition to pay off, so I needed to work. I already had a well-paying job at TTU and could continue it through the summer. But Dan responded, "I'll see what I can do."

The next thing I knew, I got a call from my old boss at Word of Life. He told me we could pay off the balance if I worked there that summer. On top of that, he said I would still have some spending money left over. I'm not sure how that all worked out, but I was very thankful for Dan's thoughtfulness. That night, my excitement barely let me sleep. I praised God for his provision and goodness. He was giving me something I desired, but I hadn't even thought about praying for it because it didn't seem possible. I was reminded again that God is powerful and sees the cares of my heart.

That summer, Dan and I worked in different areas (I at the Inn and he on the Island), but we still made time to see each other. We were both given the responsibility of being head counselors for the staff. Seeking to encourage one another, we would share our struggles in dealing with the ongoing disobedience of some staff members, which led to dismissals. We prayed for strength to lead well and graciously. We also addressed many complaints and problems that the staff had, so we prayed for compassion and wisdom. We both developed significantly in our leadership and management skills that summer.

That summer opened my eyes to a different type of ministry. Previously, my responsibilities were confined to a specific area and a limited number of people. But as a head counselor, I got a small taste of pastoral care. I heard about everything—the good and the bad—and discouragement was always at my doorstep. I knew I still needed to grow in caring for others in a pastoral way.

First Steps – Prayer

As mentioned, when Howie Williams spoke at the Inn, he encouraged us to pray for different countries that needed to hear the gospel. I started praying for Bangladesh, which corresponded with my WOL club book, and Dan leaned toward areas of Europe.

When I arrived to study missions at TTU, my professor Mickey Johnson said, "Pick a country that you think God may be leading you to." I immediately thought of Bangladesh, but he continued, "Pray for that country. Many people say God is calling them into missions, but then you ask them about where. They reply, 'I don't know.'" He wanted us to think more specifically about our futures.

"Hey, Bubar, do you think all fields are white to harvest?"

He said, "Well, what do you mean? The Scriptures say so."

"Yeah, but are all fields white all the time or only during the harvest? Like wheat or corn – they are not always white to harvest. Do you think God has a timetable for some locations?"

"Hmm, that's a good question. Look at Europe and the Soviet Union; they face major changes. I believe they are white for harvest; at least, the youth are," Dan responded.

"As I study, I lean toward the idea that not all fields are white. Just look at the fields of New York; the generations before us removed the stones from the fields to help farm production. The early settlers labored to prepare the fields and orchards. Furthermore, there appears to be a specific time for planting and sowing in agriculture. Isn't this the same spiritually?"

"Butler, concerning this, I think our generation is the one to remove the rocks, plant seeds, or even harvest among European youth. Let's just do it."

"Bubar, it must be so for Europe, the former Soviet Union, and I hope for the Muslim world. Didn't Paul mention that some of us water, and others plant, while some take in the harvest? God seems to determine the whiteness of the people's response."

"I am beginning to realize that going is not just about where the opportunity exists, but also about plowing the ground to create an opportunity," Dan replied.

He continued, "Missions today have a business mentality. Do what is productive. Only invest in responsive and productive areas; do not invest in unresponsive ones. May we not fall into this thinking."

"Remember at WOL we were challenged to pray to the Lord of the harvest to send out laborers? The problem today is that there are not enough laborers, no cultivation, and a harvest can be lost. Also, could a harvest *not* occur, due to a lack of workers?"

I continued, "In fact, look at Saudi Arabia. It's not white to harvest. No one has planted there or even removed the rocks from the soil. The passage in John 4 discusses the Samaritans, who had prophets like Elisha and partial copies of the Scriptures. Jesus said they were white for harvest."

Sensing I was preaching to the choir, Bubar said, "Butler, let's just go and preach the gospel, whether white or not."

I recalled the WOL club missionary Ken Dady, who shared these words with the kitchen staff at the Inn: "Preachers today want a ministry established. Some have to get out and start one." Both Dan and I felt God was calling us to go out and start one.

University Work

Finally, as roommates, we began a two-and-a-half-year journey where we interacted daily at TTU.

Working during university built our character. During the fall of 1986, Dan, dressed like a salesman, returned to the dorm saying, "I found a job!"

"Wow, that's great." I knew how hard it was to make ends meet. He was so thrilled to have a job and began to tell me about it. The job was door-to-door sales, something I would not wish even on my enemy. Yet Dan loved the challenge.

After a few days, I realized he neglected to say what he was selling. I'd assumed books or vacuum cleaners, but in his excitement, or perhaps embarrassment, Dan was mute about that detail. So I asked, "How did selling go?" His face brightened, and he said, "I visited an older man and made a sale."

"Bubar, what exactly did you sell?"

He responded, "A plot."

"A what?"

"I sold this older man a grave plot."

I saw the potential for wisecracks. "Really? You're selling grave plots to old people! What about reaching the youth of the world?"

"Yeah, that's my new job," He assured me stoically.

"So, how does this work?"

"Well, each day, I receive a list of individuals over 50, and when I arrive at the door, I explain the benefits of purchasing a plot early."

He continued, "Then I say, 'The reasonable price is a thoughtful investment for their heirs, and…" he paused slightly, "our company *will be the last one to let you down.*"

Managing Money

Bubarism was our common buzzword, and we often talked about what his dad said or did. Usually, significant exaggeration came into play, and these Bubarisms constantly became a subplot in our lives.

Dan learned the importance of faithfulness with finances through his dad's transparency.

His father had attended Barrington College in Rhode Island before it merged with Gordon College. The "Bubarism" was that his mother gave him money to take music or singing lessons at college.

That's how Bubar began the story.

"Your dad knows how to sing?"

"Well, no. Can you imagine my dad up there singing with the Collegians?"

"Ah, no, I cannot," I replied.

He continued, "Anyway, he took this money and bought a motorcycle."

"What money? Do you mean for the lessons?" I asked.

"Yes, he was delinquent and bought a motorcycle." Dan let out a characteristic guffaw.

"Was this the motorcycle he drove up on stage at the Island?" We laughed at the funny memory.

"No," Dan said. *"Wealth gotten by vanity shall be diminished: but he that gathereth by labour shall increase"* (Proverbs 13:11).

Although we did not discuss money extensively at university, our mindsets on the subject were similar: we wanted to be good stewards of whatever the Lord gave us.

Dan had taken this story to heart, and though he laughed about his dad's youthful folly, it made him firmer about integrity in stewardship. The fruit of his dad's openness reached my heart as well. Our college years would test and stretch us in the area of finances.

Avoiding Debt

Neither of our families thought we should be lazy while in university. We both planned to work and avoid debt.

Bubar sold cemetery plots, and for one semester, I stood on the Little Debbie's line in the middle of the night to maintain quality control for Oatmeal Cream Pies. These jobs were replaced by others, such as Dairy Queen, restaurant bakery, door monitoring, and library positions.

During the second year together, the university placed mini fridges in the dorms. I walked in with boxes of Little Debbie snacks, cases of soda, and plastics of liquid color to make into ice.

Bubar asked, "What are all these for?"

"Stuart and I are going into business. We decided to sell snacks to other students to help us stay in school."

"Well, you know I won't be the best customer because I don't eat junk food," he said bluntly.

This is how it started. During one of my financial crises, I discussed going into sales with our roommate, Stuart. Neither of us was a business major, but most of our customers were. Now, he had a car and was an ideal business partner. I told him he could transport the stuff, and I would sell it. Like me, he needed some extra cash.

Dan never complained about the constant flow of students coming in to find a snack or to coordinate a sale. Amidst the distractions in our room, he would go to the library when he needed to focus. He accepted our endeavor but knew how to delve into his study when needed.

We all worked somehow, and at times, we had more than two jobs. We found a thrill in selling to make ends meet and stay in school. Stuart and I contemplated leaving school to work for a semester or year, knowing full well that a return would be challenging.

Bubar one day announced, "Did you see that a room on the second floor is also selling snacks?" You have competition."

"Oh, really? Well, we'll see how that goes," I said.

Then Bubar noted two days later, "Did you hear what happened to your competition?"

"No, are they selling well? What are they selling now?" I inquired.

"No, the Dean of Men shut them down. That other room posted a sign on the public soda machine on the lower level, and the salesman saw it and complained to the school."

"Wow. It's a good thing we got permission beforehand!" We posted only in the dorm hallways. I was relieved that we had an accidental foresight on both counts.

"You were smart and knew your context," Bubar said.

Praise the Lord that we, non-business majors, both grossed $368 in cake sales and an additional $290 in soda sales during our final year (1987 rates, adjusted for inflation to $1,011 and $797, respectively). Enough to help with our financial shortages. Dan benefited from his occasional, "I think I will try one of those icy pops."

Despite always having soda and snacks in our room, we managed to demonstrate some self-control. Neither of us cared much for junk food, but we were motivated to make money. Also, Bubar would say about the snacks, *"He that hath no rule over his own spirit is like a city that is broken down, and without walls"* Proverbs 25:28. He loved to quote from Proverbs.

Bubar said, "Well, do you know, Butler, what the number one reason is that keeps people from going overseas?"

As a Missions major, I well knew. "Yes, I know. Debt."

We both took advantage of scholarships, on-campus work, and outside jobs to make ends meet. We never discussed how much his parents contributed to his bill, but his brother Dave also studied there. So I can imagine their help was sufficient but still limited.

This financial debt — a hindrance to missions — propelled me, but I also faced another inner challenge. During high school, my dad was quite clear about not providing me with financial assistance during college. He wanted all his kids to go but said more than once that he would not pay for it. I internalized my dad's comments as a personal challenge. I can recall at least once responding to him with, "Don't worry, *I will graduate debt-free.* I made it a matter of prayer and faced multiple economic crises while at TTU, but they forced me to depend on my heavenly Father. Praise the Lord; He enabled both of us to graduate debt-free.

Both Dan and I had the underlying philosophy of trusting in the Lord, not finances, while using our efforts to help in how God provided.

■■

Chapter Six - Dating and Other Horror Stories

No one likes to share dating experiences that fail. However, as young Christians search for "the one" God may have for them, they are bound to make blunders. The struggle in going to the mission field frequently centers on the relationships they are involved in or will have.

"Butler, God provided a wife for Adam, and he will for us, too."

"Yeah, but Adam's choices were already narrowed down!"

"It's like Joseph Stowell said: We don't have to go around beating the bushes to find a wife. God will provide," he reminisced.

"Oh, yeah, go to sleep, and God will bring a wife," I said sarcastically.

"Well, we sleep and wait for God...but we sleep with one eye open," he concluded.

Having committed our lives to missions, we felt the weight of choosing someone who was also called, and time seemed shorter as we made our way through university.

"Look at Johnny Reimer and Steve Theis; they went overseas as singles for Word of Life, at least at first. If these men can do it, so can Danny Bubar."[26]

This was not just a one-off comment. These men's lives encouraged Dan to take a step of faith and go overseas single. He also said no girl would stop him from serving the Lord. Despite his desire to get married, he would not wait for a girl to come along. Nor would he make a rash choice that would hijack God's call on his life. He would go to the field and trust the Lord to lead.

While this was our self-talk, we began noticing others and their situations. During our university years, I kept bumping into individuals who had changed their focus from missions because they were dating or getting married to someone who wasn't interested in going overseas. I recall one guy who said, "I wanted to go the Middle East; then I got married." I now realize that God's ways of bringing people together are far more complex, but our single-mindedness helped us focus our lives on the field during our first terms. We had a healthy fear of going in the wrong direction.

Praying for your future wife

During the summer of 1982, one of the speakers mentioned the importance of praying daily for your future spouse. He used Genesis 2:22, "God ... brought her to the man." He stressed the importance of committing this process to the Lord. So obediently, in case it was God's will for me to marry, I wrote my future spouse in my quiet time. I started to pray for her and for God to prepare us for each other. I rewrote this request each year as I worked through the WOL diary.

When I started this practice in 1982, a problem arose. My future wife was not a believer and wouldn't become one for another six years. So, while I was praying, thinking she was a Christian, she was actually moving towards atheism and would have intensely disliked someone like me. God is powerful. I did not know the magnitude of what He was doing while I prayed.

The Word of Life atmosphere lends itself to dating — so many teens, all wanting to get to know each other — and Dan and my many summers at WOL provided some very healthy relationships. In 1983, one teen girl I dated seemed like a perfect match. Yet, in the fall, she was heading off to Tennessee Temple University (TTU), and I was still in high school. I was warned that university changes people. Many couples broke up when one was in university but the other was still in high school.

Realizing this while praying, I felt the best thing to do was give the relationship to the Lord. On our last day together during the summer, we parted with the freedom to see how the Lord would lead each of us. I prayed that if the Lord wanted us together, he would bring us back together. She felt confused about why I was stopping the dating relationship. Yet, in prayer, I felt the need to give the relationship to the Lord, trusting him to work out the timing and direction.

A few months later, I arranged to visit TTU and see what life was like there, considering the possibility of studying there. My father had a trip planned down that way, so he dropped me off for a two-night stay. My first night on campus, I tried to ring my former girlfriend down to the lobby. Her roommate said she was out on a date. Ironically, when I arrived at TTU two years later, she was married. With no regrets, I thanked the Lord for how he leads.

God's Timing

During the summers, Dan had no serious girlfriend. He had friends and, at times, took "safe" girls to banquets, but he did not have any serious pursuits during his teenage years. However, he repeatedly committed this vital area to the Lord.

The Scriptures state there is a time to love (Ecc. 3:8). The Lord will lead on his timetable. One event during the summer of 1983 will remain with me for the rest of my life. At the Inn, the evening before the Billy Speer concert, Harry Bollback, co-founder of Word of Life, felt inspired to dedicate a song he had written for his wife, dedicating this evening to a couple celebrating their anniversary.

In his jovial manner, Harry humbly debased himself by saying he is not a good musician or a poet. "Now I can't sing, but who cares anyhow, ladies and gentlemen? ... I wrote this for my wife on our 25th wedding anniversary… I've got a terrible voice, but I am going to sing this anyhow. Now, the last time I played and sang, everybody cried, but I sang anyhow, who cares… Now you will know from the beginning that I am not a good soloist… This takes courage to do, believe me." His self-deprecating humor always amused the crowd and drew compassion.

The beautiful words he wrote and sang are as follows:

In the springtime of my life the flowers came when first I heard your name. Ever since that day and in every way, it has never been the same. And you became my wife in the springtime of my life.

Then our love was kissed by summer sun as more and more we were one. And though seasons change you remain for our love has just begun. And you were my wife in the summer of my life.

So, the leaves will fade and fall and it will not be long but we'll still sing our song. Of the happy days and the happy years, for our love is true and strong. And you'll be my wife in the autumn of my life.

Springtime, Summertime or Autumn. Flowers, rain or snow. It's always springtime in my life since you became my wife.[27]

His sincerity and love for his wife spoke to my heart. I bought a cassette of the concert so I would always have this song as a treasure. It taught me what love might feel like and how love grows through the passing of time together.

At that point, Harry and Mille had been married "only" 35 years, not even half the time their marriage endured, which lasted until their passing in 2021.

A big part of Dan's and my TTU experience was our dating adventures, or, more accurately, the lack thereof. This affected me more than Dan since he always seemed to accept rejection much better than I did — not to say he was unfazed, but in his stoic manner, he stood fast.

Case Study on Dan's Dating

I remember Dan being quite interested in one girl. I am writing this as a case study to show Dan's attitude toward dating. I mean no harm to anyone, but to show that in all our difficulties in dating, we need to align with God's will for us. Dan was persistent in what he thought he should do and, in this case, who he should pursue.

"Bubar, who are you taking to the concert?" I asked.

To deflect the uncomfortable topic, Dan often said, "You are funny.... Looking!"

"No, really. Have you considered asking someone?"

"Well, you know, Butler, we should be able to find a date since looks aren't everything.... They are the only thing."

I grinned, continuing with his deflection. "Well, based on our looks, we don't have much chance."

Dan liked a lovely student named Anne. Her connection to Word of Life and her Christian family background meant that Dan had hit his criteria jackpot.

Many guys were pursuing Anne, but Dan was up for the challenge. One day, we saw just how much competition he had. We had just settled at a table for breakfast in the bustling dining room. Anne strolled in, and we saw her take a seat near us. She placed her books down to reserve her spot, as was typical, and she went to get her food.

Once she returned, one of her admirers confidently approached her and politely asked if he could sit near her. She graciously agreed; she was always so kind to others. Her good manners often led men to believe she reciprocated their feelings. Her admirer smiled across from her, placed his books, and then walked off to grab his food.

Meanwhile, another student was walking in and noticed the supposedly empty seat near Anne. As he got closer, he must have seen the books purposefully placed before her, but they did not deter him. He asked Anne if he could sit by her, and she nodded politely, smiling. He beamed at her, pushed aside the other man's books, and placed his books in their place. He strutted away to get his food before he could see the shock on her face.

Anne looked around, panic-stricken, fearing the next suitor. She quickly called a girlfriend to sit by her, hoping to deter more guys. Eventually, the first guy got back and saw his books displaced. He was perplexed but swiftly pushed the other books aside and sat across from Anne. Soon after, the second guy came back with his tray of food. Noticing the shift in the seating arrangement, he called out the other guy for taking his seat. Dan, Jeff Street, and I watched the whole scenario, thinking it hysterical. Dan was thankful he was not among those who had tried to save a seat across from Anne that day.

Nevertheless, Dan was ever confident in his pursuit of Anne. He always seemed to feel she would be open to dating him. Over and over, he would find ways to show his interest. It became a constant joke between Dan and me. Finally, he realized he wasn't getting anywhere, and after all of Dan's self-inflicted torture, someone informed him that Anne saw him only as a friend. Women often said this about us: "He is a great guy, but I only like him as a friend." It was always a compliment and a slap to our ego simultaneously. Luckily, Dan handled this rejection well. I, on the other hand, despite numerous brush-offs, still struggled to handle them as well as Dan did.

It helped Dan that his standards were so stringent. He only wanted to date someone who came from a Christian family. He held to this standard firmly despite my jibes. "What am I? Should women avoid me because I'm not from a Christian home?"

Dan preferred Word of Life women. Yet, there was one girl I remember that Dan was interested in who was not connected to Word of Life. He didn't even know her, but she was always studying in the library, which appealed to Dan because he was always there too.

At first, he was hesitant since she was not a "Word of Lifer." However, I rejoiced that Dan was even considering loosening his standards in that area, so I encouraged him. He was wondering about asking her to a music recital at the university.

"Just do it, Danny. Go ask her!" I encouraged him. He took a deep breath and, with renewed confidence, walked towards her studying cubby. As he approached, the girl kept her eyes glued to her books, but Dan was not deterred.

"Hello, my name is Daniel Bubar. What's your name?" The girl looked up at him suddenly. Her face was shocked, and she let out a quiet "Oh." She seemed quite perplexed and disturbed to be conversing with Dan during her studies. They had a brief conversation, but she continued to glance at her books and offer brief replies. Beginning to feel uncomfortable, he quickly ended the awkward conversation and rushed back towards me.

"What happened? Did you ask?" I looked at him with anticipation.

"No," Dan said, shoulders slumped.

"Why not? What happened?" I pressed.

"Well..." Dan sighed. "I opened with, 'Hello, my name is Daniel Bubar,' and from there, it went downhill. She looked so taken aback and shocked that I would even approach her. I couldn't bring myself to ask her."

"Oh, that's too bad. Her loss." I felt terrible that his one encounter with a non-WOL girl ended so miserably. Eventually, we were both able to laugh off the situation. I would tease Daniel with his opening line, "Hello, my name is Daniel Bubar" — which we learned was a scary intro for some and how not to ask a girl out.

***

My Case Study: Hopeless Attraction

While Dan's interests were few and short-lived, I pursued many different girls. However, there was one girl in particular that I continued to like throughout my years at TTU. Even when I'd temporarily changed my focus, I couldn't shake my attraction to her. I knew, deep down, though, that God did not want us to be together.

God was calling me to full-time ministry, whereas the woman I was interested in wanted to minister in public schools, which I rationalized was like going overseas. I convinced myself that this was a non-issue — that she would change once she was with me. As a planner, I wanted to check the "found my future wife" box.

But God had his own plans for me, and they would happen in his timing. Now and then, I was hit with clarity, realizing I needed to wait for God. One night, I was talking with Dan about my relational struggles.

Our conversation often mentioned Adam beating the bushes in the garden to look for his spouse, and God bringing Eve to him while he slept. Of course, Dan's remark about praying with one eye open always made the cut.

On one occasion, Dan looked at me seriously. " 'A man's heart deviseth his way, but the Lord directeth his steps.'[28] We shouldn't just sit by lazily. It's good to plan and act, but we must hold onto those plans loosely, knowing that God will direct where things go." I nodded at Dan's words. It was holding onto the plans loosely that I had trouble with.

He continued with another proverb about making wise decisions and then said, "Favour is deceitful, and beauty is vain: but a woman that feareth the LORD, she shall be praised" (Proverbs 31:30). He seemed to encourage me not to look on the outward appearance but to find a woman who loves God and is called to go overseas.

I appreciated those conversations with Dan. They helped me process where I needed to grow and held me accountable.

My turmoil was evident in my journal entry one night: *"What do you do when your love for one hinders your direction for God? One's flesh and heart have a lot of strength to oppose the Spirit's leading in one's life. It is so easy to follow after your desires. But will that lead to a wise decision — an excellent choice? A thousand times, no! Only a heart sensitive to God's leading in fellowship with his Lord, in complete obedience to the Word, and their mind stayed upon and meditating on the Lord, [this] can make an excellent choice in the area of one's heart desire."* I felt a constant tug to follow my heart's desires and push God's word and wisdom away. It is an easy thing to do. After all, the serpent's lie was beautiful, delicious, and partial truth. Dan knew that, in times of love interest, he needed to focus on God even more diligently. Logically, I knew it too, but, as one does, I had to learn the hard way, with only heartbreak and vain results.

Dan would push me towards God's word, and I meditated on the verse, "My flesh and my heart may fail, but God is the strength of my heart and my portion forever" (Psalm 73:26, NASB95). Although my heart led me astray, I was encouraged to know that I could count on God's strength. When I relied on him more, He gave me more peace.

Dan saw my turmoil and the rollercoaster of my emotions when we spoke late in the day. He heard the questions and frustrations. Through it all, he showed compassion for my struggles and took it upon himself to resolve the issue. He spoke to her honestly to gauge her feelings about me, and she told him that she respected me but only wanted to be friends.

When Dan figured this out, he came to pick me up from work. "What are you doing here?" I asked.

"I'm taking you for a bite to eat," he said.

Now, I know he cared a lot for me because Dan was always very frugal with his money.

As he treated me to Hardees, he broke the news: "She only wants to be friends… She is not the one the Lord has for you."

My heart felt sick, but having Dan with me softened the blow. He counseled me and prayed with me. He reminded me once again of Psalm 73:25-26, "Whom have I in heaven but thee? and besides you, I desire nothing on earth. My flesh and my heart faileth: but God is the strength of my heart, and my portion forever" (KJV). I took comfort in knowing that God is all I need and deserves all my desires.

I felt forlorn as my heart was healing, but Dan stayed by my side, patiently offering prayer, encouragement, and truth. One night, I was in tears over the significant loss (so I thought), and I went somewhere in solitude to think, pray, and mourn. Soon, I felt humbled and passionate, wanting to keep God as number one in my life. I told God I didn't want to be more committed to an earthly attraction than to him, asking him to show me where this was the case.

Eventually, Dan found me where I had wandered off to. We sat in the stairwell, with the tiny light of the moon illuminating our faces. He counseled me more and prayed with me. He comforted me by sharing the verse, "The Lord will perfect that which concerneth me" (Psalm 138:8, KJV). I remembered God's sovereignty and his care for me. He would work it out. I felt peace about the situation, knowing I could trust God.

Eventually, the object of my hopeless attraction started dating a guy I had introduced her to. And only four months later, he proposed to her, and she said yes. I laughed to myself when this happened. This guy had accomplished in four months what I had tried to achieve for four years. I was reminded that God was at work. He kept me out of that relationship and closed the doors, worked out their issues perfectly, and brought them together. At the time, Dan tried to comfort me by saying she was rebounding from me, but we both knew that was not the case.

With all my dating failures at TTU, I realized, after some calculations, that I was the last guy a girl would date before meeting the one they eventually married. I went on one-time dates for

University events, but nothing too serious. Yet I counted six girls that married the next guy they dated. I coped with the hardship of so many dating failures by joking with Dan that I had prepared them for their husbands. We were both bitten by some form of the hopeless attraction bug, which the Lord used to get us where He wanted us to be.

I praise God that he kept me from serious relationships back then. I was still growing and, truthfully, I was seeking a relationship that would benefit me rather than considering whom I would love and care for.

Chapter Seven - WOL Dan at TTU

Dan exuded Word of Life while at university, and, for both of us, the influence was not something we could brush aside at TTU. Despite being 18 hours away from the WOL property, living with Dan still felt like we were at a WOL event. He became an enthusiast and a WOL ambassador for the Chattanooga area.

Besides comforting my broken heart, Dan's time was filled by working with the youth. When he started at TTU, he quickly got involved with the Word of Life ministries in the area. I tried many angles to get him to broaden his scope beyond Word of Life.

"If you only see one way of thinking your whole life, you will never be challenged and will never grow." I appealed to his ministry ethics, thinking I'd finally caught him.

"Butler, look at us. Where are we?" Dan looked at me expectantly.

"In our dorm room?" I questioned.

"Yeah, yeah, but I mean the university. This is TTU, not Word of Life. I *am* here to broaden my perspective." Dan looked at me intently. "I agree that never being challenged in your views can cause you to be weak. But trust me, Butler, I get enough challenge from you alone!" I smiled at that comment, slowly shaking my head.

"Well, you may be here, but you're making it into a Word of Life haven for yourself. You hang out with Word of Life people, join the Word of Life ministries, and implement all the Word of Life things."

"I want to do ministry alongside Word of Life, so why shouldn't I? And you?" Dan said, pointing straight at my face. "Aren't you proof that not everyone who attends Word of Life thinks the same?"

Thankfully, our challenging banter never led to any anger or bitterness between us; instead, we felt sharpened by each other.

Knowing One's Audience

Dan and I started a group to pray for other countries, inspired by the prayer bands we led at BI. I had the means to do this, too, because in my first week on campus, I inadvertently became vice president of the Students Missions Fellowship (SMF) group. Some of my WOL friends, including Junior Farrell, who was on my bus at Perth Bible, snagged me to help with the SMF used book sale, held at the beginning of every school year. I was introduced to Jim Laidlaw, the president of SMF, and attended the first meeting, along with other Word of Lifers. They needed a VP, and somehow, I was appointed. I was shocked but excited to be involved. I realized I still had much to learn.

The SMF met twice a week and had special activities. When Dan arrived the following year, I became the president of SMF, and with Dan's encouragement, my first action was to start prayer bands at the university. Our WOL background influenced this; the groups took off with small gatherings, praying for different parts of the world. Additionally, our mission project supported five students heading out for summer missions, including some former BI students.

In Jan. 1987, I listed Jack Wyrtzen, Bob & Patty Fischer, Paul Bubar, Richard Corley, and John Lawrence as potential speakers for our small group. All but Richard Corley were connected with Word of Life, but a few years later, I would end up working with him in the Middle East during my first term overseas (He also was a TTU Alumni).

"So, Dan, can you help me with some of these people? I know the Fischers and John Lawrence, but what about your dad and Jack Wyrtzen?"

"Well, Butler, you know they have things planned for many months and sometimes years in advance?"

"Yes, I know, but I trust you to pull some strings," I joked.

"Okay, Okay, let me see what I can do."

Well, his father spoke when he came through, and other WOL missionaries, such as John Lawrence from France, also passed through and spoke. When Jack Wyrtzen arrived, he addressed the entire student body.

We were bringing our WOL flavor to TTU, and for many WOLBI grads, this wasn't a problem. WOL'ers are known for their enthusiasm, especially during certain songs. Harry Bollback always encouraged a shout-out of one's year at the BI, particularly after the song "Be a Missionary." So, when we sang this song in our meetings, any WOL'er can imagine what happened.

At the song's end, the WOL'ers looked at each other, not wanting to be outdone by their upperclassmen, so the final shout was always a loud blur of graduation years in the '80s.

Though I'd enjoyed this at WOLBI, it did not sit well with me at TTU. Missions are all about relating to others and, as the Apostle Paul said, "becoming all things to all men." Here, the WOL'ers' enthusiasm, which the SMF staff loved, actually divided the group and alienated the non-WOL'ers. We needed some cultural adaptation.

For most WOL'ers, TTU was a total culture shock, and they felt out of place in this strict Baptist university. Having a common bond brought comfort and companionship. None of us wanted to forfeit that.

So the proposal was to do a different shout-out. At the song's end, we would shout "Student Missions Fellowship" and then either the present this year or one's TTU graduation year. It was a small way of uniting the group and practicing cultural adaptation.

Flaunting our affiliation with WOL continued to be a challenge. I recall going to get ice cream with five other students. Three of us were WOL'ers, and we started to chat about WOL—how much we loved the place, the events, and our mutual friends. We went on for some time, unaware of the growing tension. The camaraderie was great — for three of us — until one of the other three suggested we change the topic. However, the enthusiasm for WOL continued to spill over. The non-WOL'ers were getting peeved, to the point that one later remarked they never wanted to spend time with anyone who went to WOL.

We were sometimes unaware of our surroundings and how to incorporate others into a shared enthusiasm. This reminded me of Ecclesiastes 10:1, where the dead flies make the perfume stink. Our enthusiasm became an odious smell to others, and we needed wisdom in how we discussed a shared experience with others.

In our international cultural studies, we needed to find ways to bring ourselves into our surroundings, including learning to speak another's language and understanding their values to initiate relationship. Despite being fellow students, these object lessons affected me.

Dan and WOL Local Ministry

So, while I mainly worked with the student ministry on campus, Dan worked a lot with the WOL local church ministry.

I wasn't with him on his various expeditions, but I constantly heard stories about their adventures from one of our buddies, Jeff Street. Dan, Jeff, and James Boyer teamed up for this local ministry. Since I wasn't a part of this ministry, I guess Dan needed another Jeff around.

In the summer of 1987, before Jeff Street arrived at TTU, he served with the basketball camp on the Island, where the ministry focused on training and competition. Jeff Street shared his intro to Dan:

"I got sent to the Island, and I was 18. Dan was our unit leader. I have no memory of my co-counselor or anyone else there.

"But I remember that Dan invited us to the A-frame where they lived. We all sat on the deck, and I am sure he gave us some lemonade or something. And he tried to tell us what we were doing wrong, how we were not doing a good job, or to the point of that….

"I remember him saying, 'This time there is no guilt, no guilt... ah-ha,' like how Dan would laugh, trying to make his point without being too harsh, which overall, in retrospect, as an old guy now, is a fairly good way to go about it. He was trying to get his point across and was not too heavy-handed. So he said, 'You guys have not been doing this,' telling us what we did wrong. 'This time, no guilt, just shame, just shame, but next time, if you do not do it. It is going to be guilt… ah-ha' with his laugh.

"I was sitting there thinking, *Wow, this is really strange because I greatly respected Paul Bubar as a BI student. I only knew him from afar, like in chapel.* He was one of the top five Christians in my life at that point. So now I am thinking, *Wow, this is his kid?*"

With this basis, Jeff showed up with TTU for another encounter with Dan, he recalls:

"I remember going to Chauncy-Goode for a chapel service. It was in August and early in the semester, and I remember seeing Dan in the lobby with a crowd of guys; he was very animated and talking. As you know, he was surrounded by his gang of pals with whom he is comfortable. With…feeling good, yukking it up, and very comfortable in his environment. I was very uncomfortable in the TTU environment, especially my first few weeks… I remember looking over and thinking, oh yeah, that's Dan Bubar, and I remember his conversation about no guilt, just shame, *but next time, guilt!* … I didn't think I would get to know him much as he was *out of my league. He is an important kid from a big and important dad and looks like he is in the loop around here.*"

Despite these bumps in the road, these guys got together. Dan and Jeff once brought the local church youth group to a Word of Life basketball marathon. They loaded up several buses to head to the event. Once the event was over, they were ready to head back towards TTU.

"Do you have all your people?" the youth pastor called out before they were ready to leave.

"We don't have Don with us," Jeff told Dan. Don Schamberg was another TTU student from Schroon Lake helping with the ministry.

"No, Don has got to be with us," Dan quickly spurted out. Jeff looked at him in confusion, knowing Don was nowhere in sight.

"How do you know he is with us?" Jeff asked, giving Dan the benefit of the doubt.

"Street." Dan looked at Jeff seriously, panic covering his face. "Don has got to be with us. He has to be. The pastor wants us to leave, and he has to go. We have to go now." Dan's eyes were wide.

"But Dan," Jeff interjected, "I just looked at the other bus, and he wasn't there. Everyone else is there, but not Don."

"No," Dan shook his head, his brows furrowed, "he has got to be on that bus. He has to be."

Before Jeff could bring some clarity and sanity to Dan, the pastor called out from the front, "Are we good to go?" His words only added to Dan's urgency, and Dan quickly popped his thumb up to signal that everything was good to go. The pastor said goodbye to the bus. Jeff looked at Dan in shock, hoping that somehow Dan was right and Don had hopped on the bus at the last moment.

The bus started to move forward, and with a two-hour drive ahead of them, Jeff knew that if something were to happen, it had to happen now.

"Hey Dan," Jeff prodded, "Don is not on that bus."

"He's got to be!" Dan rushed on. "He's got to be!" Jeff sighed and shrugged, thinking, "All right, we will see."

The two-hour drive passed, and finally, they were at TTU. The other bus had already arrived and dispersed, keeping Don's whereabouts a mystery.

Jeff suggested they check Don's dorm room to see if he was back, so they walked over to his room. Lo and behold, Don was nowhere to be seen. Finally, the two went to Dan's room and saw a note I had posted on the door.

While they were out, someone called the dorm phone, and since I was heading out to work, I posted a note for him to see: "You forgot Don. He will meet you at the Marriott Mall."

Dan could not believe it and quickly declared, "We need to go and get him." They rushed to get in the car and headed back to the mall for two hours. They talked the whole way there, helping the trip go by quickly.

Jeff and Dan walked into the mall's right-side entrance and began searching for Don.

"Yoo-hoo, I'm here!" Don called to them from above. They looked up and saw him on the upper level and quickly headed up to meet him.

"Have you been able to eat?" Dan asked Don, worry lacing his voice.

"Oh yeah, I ate a steak earlier with the pastor," Don replied happily. Dan and Jeff stared at him as hunger gnawed at their stomachs.

"Well," Dan started, and his stomach grumbled as if on cue, "We haven't eaten in a while and are famished, so maybe we can grab some McDonald's or something." Jeff nodded enthusiastically.

They quickly drove to McDonald's and headed inside. They pulled out their wallets to see what the budget was, but to their surprise, they only had four dollars between the three of them. They looked at the measly four dollars in misery.

"Let's scour the car. I'm sure there's some change lying around in there somewhere," Dan chipped in with an encouraging smile. They all rushed to the car, full of hope. They looked between the seats and on the floors, but somehow, the car was clean of any coins. Dan, who was usually messy, out of all people, suddenly had a clean car at the worst of times.

Deflated, they headed back into McDonald's, but Dan was determined to make the most of the situation. He faced it head-on, declaring, "We will just buy what we can." So they made their order, figuring out the prices of everything as they went and trying to squeeze as much as possible out of the four dollars.

Once their food was ready, the cashier plopped a huge handful of Monopoly cards onto their tray, part of a new promotion.[29] These cards sometimes contained rewards for McDonald's, so they all thought it was great that they got so many.

They sat down without food and began opening the cards.

"Free Big Mac!" Don exclaimed with a large grin.

"This one says free shake," Dan added.

Jeff opened another one, ready to join the chorus of excitement: "A free small Coke!" Jeff waved the card in front of the others. They all grinned and praised God for his provision and goodness. They started with four dollars but walked away with eleven dollars' worth of food.

Knowing God worked it out, the day ended well despite the earlier chaos. They had a funny story to tell afterward, and no one got hurt. Additionally, Dan received a humble reminder that only God can speak things into existence.

Making Lemonade out of Lemons

I heard another story from Jeff Street that gave me more insight into Dan's ministry during college. I could hardly believe it, but I suppose, by that point, I shouldn't have been surprised by Dan's tenacity.

In his WOL local church activities, he visited nearby clubs in Georgia, which were run by WOL missionaries Mike Ellis and Junior Farrell. While Chattanooga had few clubs in those days, Georgia had many because Mike Calhoun had previously developed many in that state before taking over the directorship of the Clubs in Schroon Lake.

Nearby in Alabama were TTU chapels that students would fill or pastor to gain ministry experience. I recall a chapel I preached in one time. It was a small group of fewer than fifteen, and most likely, all attendees were somehow related to one another. So, ministry in these chapels existed, but it faced many challenges, including small numbers and minimal youth attendance. Despite this, Dan used this network to develop new clubs through these chapels and churches.

One weekend, Dan, James Boyer, and Jeff Street headed off to Gadsden, Alabama, where there was a youth group but no WOL clubs. Dan said, "We are showing them why they need WOL clubs and how great WOL is, *as we are all WOL'ers.*" So, they drove down to this area about 90 miles south of Chattanooga.

When they arrived, the TTU chapel pastor said, "I'm sorry, our youth group is only three people, and none of them showed up. So sorry to make you guys drive all the way down here."

Then Dan said, "Where are the kids from the church?"

The pastor said, "Well, I was hoping they would bring friends, but none of the youth showed up."

Dan responded, "Well, let's go and get them from where they live."

The pastor, amused by this, said, "Okay, follow me."

They knocked on the door of one of the youths. When asked about the youth, his mother replied, "Oh, well, he's still sleeping." "

It was 11 o'clock in the morning. Then Dan responded, "That's okay, we'll wake him up!" The mother said, "Sure, go ahead."

Jeff Street, the voice of sanity, asked, "So we are going into the bedroom of these kids we have never seen before? Are you sure?"

Dan, without wavering, walked into the room. The kid looked up with a complete bedhead, only to turn back over.

Dan approached the bed, "Haha!" and started to shake the kid. The others, James, Jeff, and the pastor, stood and watched, amazed.

"Come on, get up! Get up! We're having a special activity. Come on! Get up!" Dan, breathlessly hyped, continued, "Come! We've got to go. It'll be great!"

He gently shook the teen and even started pulling him out of bed, "Get up, Get up! We are going to have this youth activity."

The teen, energized by this turn of events, woke up and started to get ready. Dan quizzed him, "What friends do you have? Let's find your friends!"

So, they went around to more homes and persuaded other teens to join in, ending up with eleven kids at the youth event.

James was slated to preach the gospel, while others, such as Robin Brooks, stayed at the church to prepare for the outreach. When James preached, he said, "If you have never prayed that prayer of salvation, you need to go into the next room." At that point, all eleven teens got up and went to the room.

Dan and the other WOL'ers were thrilled to see so many people turning to the Lord. Then James asked one of the kids why he was in the room, and the kid replied, "I thought you said that if you have ever prayed that prayer, you should go into this room." Then he asked another youth, and he said the same thing. Whoops! James said, "Oh well, I messed up. Let's all go back into the main room."

At that point, Jeff saw a 13-year-old kid and asked him what he thought. The kid said, "No, I thought he said if you never, not if you ever. He said, 'If you never prayed.'" So Jeff stayed with him and led him to the Lord.

Later, James said, "Oh, the whole thing was such a bomb, but at least one youth accepted the Lord." It was all because of Dan's motivation: *Let's go, let's go into their bedrooms. We do not need to know these kids. We just go in and wake them up."*

A long-time WOLer, Wayne Lewis[30], once said something I will call the philosophy of WOL clubs: "Having fun is winning the right to reach young people with Jesus." In Gadsden, Dan created an opportunity out of a disappointing situation. He was always ready to employ initiative and creativity to make lemonade out of lemons. Dan walked and ministered by faith. He took Dr. Stephen Olford's words seriously, to "Take opportunities to share the gospel, but more so, make opportunities." Dan did not want the day wasted and ensured that the youth would have the chance to hear the message. Most likely, these now-grown teenagers recall the day a crazy WOL'er showed up in their bedrooms.

Although I didn't get to join Dan on these ministry adventures, I was always glad to hear the stories.

Buzzword Debate

The best part about rooming with Dan was the constant banter we had about calling and the type of ministry to dedicate our lives to.

A call is the desire of God's heart present in a person's mind. At least, that is how Mickey Johnson, my Missions professor at TTU, defined it.[31] As believers, God calls us to a life of sanctification and discipleship. Our initial call is to repentance and salvation, but after that, what we do is labeled a call.

"Butler, why don't you come with me and work with Word of Life?"

"Bubar, you know I love Word of Life, but I sense my call is something different."

"God has called all of us to go and preach the gospel. The youth of the world are waiting to hear. Come join us in the next new adventure."

I offered, "We both are called to go, but I think we are called to do different things. You see yourself with Word of Life."

"Well, you know, my whole life, it's been Word of Life," he said.

"And my call is to go where there is no church. When I look at Word of Life, I see them partnering with churches. They don't go where there is no church. I want to church plant."

At this point, I tried a different approach that I heard from others to convince him that God focused more on church planting than parachurch ministries. "Look at Romans 15:20. I aspire to preach the gospel, not where Christ is already known by name, *so I would not build on another person's foundation.* Also, when talking to Peter, Jesus said he would build his church, so church planting aligns with Jesus in his mission."

"Church planting is a buzzword," Dan responded, quoting his father.

"A buzzword, what do you mean?" I wondered aloud.

"You know, when there is a trend, and everybody wants to do that. At one point, parachurch work was the rave, but now church planting." Dan continued, "Of course, Jesus' goal was to build the church, but that is not just through physically building a church. The church comprises all believers, so anything that brings unbelievers to salvation is an act that builds the church. Word of Life utilizes its clubs, Bible Institute, and camps to reach the unsaved; when they are saved, they become part of the church. Both are part of building the church. Word of Life plants more churches than you think."

I sat thinking for a moment, knowing he was right. "Okay, fine. You are right on that," I finally responded. "But it's through hearing the gospel that God saves people, so we must go to the places where no church exists. In some locations, no one is preaching the word to the unsaved. How can they hear the word?"

"Going to unreached places is vital," Dan clarified. "We need people to start preaching the word in places that have never heard it, but neither calling is greater. What separates the unbeliever in a place with no church and the unbeliever who lives down the road from a church? Before God, they are both unbelievers who need Christ. They both need someone to minister to them. God needs people doing both types of ministries."

I nodded at him in complete agreement. Conversations like this made me realize that individual calls differ as well as the needs. One person may feel strongly about ministering in one way, and another about a different way, yet God is the Author of both methods.

"A buzzword, huh? I guess you had this discussion with your father?" I asked.

"My dad is wise and often sees the trends. After church planting had its day, another trend will dominate missions."[32]

For each of us our wills and hopes were set so we could not convince each other to change minds or paths.

Then I said, "I suppose that *he who is convinced against his will is of the same opinion still*." Our university professor Steve Winget had spoken these words concerning debating cults in our World Religions class.

I loved having these conversations with Dan because they united us despite our differences. We were on the same team. The agency

I would join set up laborers in areas where no church existed. Bubar was called to reach youth who had access to a local fellowship of believers. His was a church-based ministry, while mine led me to settings without church access.

Desire to Serve

When thinking about our dorm room debates on missions, we both could recall multiple types of ministry we did. I recall preaching on the streets of New York City or Toronto with Open Air Campaigners. We both enjoyed the open-air method because it gave us courage on the streets. Our prayers leaned toward something new, such as being part of a team building a new ministry foundation.

The WOLBI Missions conference in 1985 and the yearly one at TTU challenged many to think about new locations to minister. I considered giving attention to planting churches in non-church areas. Going south to Chattanooga had given us evidence of the massive number of churches in the States. Sharing the gospel there was interesting. Most people thought they were already Christians, and almost everyone who didn't attend church had a story to explain why they did not want to go back. We both desired a lesser-reached area.

What was the turning point for Bubar? What was the turning point for me?

One day, Dan said, " 'Delight yourself in the LORD, and he will give you the desires of your heart' (Psalm 37:4). Butler, when we delight in Him, He will give us our desires."

"So does that mean we will go married to the field?" I asked.

"Well, I'm not sure about that, but my heart desires to serve with Word of Life. I think God places these desires in our hearts. What do you think?" Dan stated.

"Well, the Lordship of Christ centers every believer's calling. However, the specifics of what or how to do something for God seem to vary for each person. I can't judge how God works, and I don't want to minimize anyone's life calling. God may work differently in each of us. I'm sensing a more non-Word of Life approach."

I continued, "Do you think God leads people through a desire for adventure? Are we going because we love adventure?"

95

He responded, "I had so much fun growing up on the Island and later working there. Seeing the changed lives in the middle of it was a lot of fun. That speaks to me."

I mused, "Every summer when I was young, my parents would take us on a road trip. We traveled to Prince Edward Island, Montana, and Florida, and I loved seeing new places. How or why I sensed adventure, stuffed for hours in the back of a VW bug, is beyond me. Or our Chevrolet Impala, which started billowing smoke when we pulled up to a KOA camp office near St. Louis. Yet somehow, these trips gave me the desire to explore and see new places."

I concluded, "God seems to use our experiences and circumstances to direct us." Dan nodded in agreement.

My 1987 Summer

The summer of 1987 was pivotal in determining our future paths. That summer, I took a training course in NYC to learn how to work with Muslims while Dan worked on the Island as a counselor. He became more assured that he would only serve with the ministry he grew up with. That summer, he met Jeff Street, who later joined the WOL church ministry at TTU.

Before we departed for the summer, Dan wrote in my 1987 yearbook,

"I am proud to have you as possibly my best friend. You have been an example and encouragement to me this year. Even though our schedules often conflicted, you found the time to encourage me when I needed it. Too bad you won't be running the 'Butler Bakery' this summer... Have a good time in NY City and don't forget to find a wife.

This year at Temple has truly been a good year. Next year at TTU can be even better. Won't it be fun to see who our new roommate will be? I'll be looking for you July 2 at WOL. We'll have some fun. It will be exciting to discover how the Lord directs us in the years to come. Please pray for me often as you know I need it. I'll pray for you this summer also. Your friend, Daniel Bubar"

Interestingly, my training took place at the Hawthorne Gospel Church, where Jack Wyrtzen had spent his early days. The church had a heart for evangelism. While there, we lived in local homes, and I was in the heart of Queens, just a few miles from where Jack was born. Our outreach was to Muslims, and all the contacts I met were Afghans.

Getting to Know Persians

In my training, we were given addresses with Muslim names. We had no idea if they were at that address or not. My experience of NYC was open-air ministry where we'd seen resistance to whatever we said about the gospel. My partner for the summer, Dave, and I felt unsure what would happen.

We found one of the first addresses listed and applied the method they recommended.

"A-salamu alaikum." I said.

The man at the door responded, "Come on in. Please come on in."

As we entered, he said, "Please take off your shoes here and come sit down." His enthusiasm stunned us, but we followed his instructions and said nothing. We followed him into his living room, and he sat us down. Then, he and another Afghan found some cookies to bring in on a plate.

After putting the tea on, he finally sat and said, "Who are you? Are you Muslim?"

"Actually, we are studying Islam and are interested in learning more about your religion," I said.

Dave added, "In our studies, we are supposed to visit Muslims and ask them questions."

Here, in the heart of NYC, these men opened their doors to us, and we proceeded to get to know these dear Afghans who fled from Afghanistan because of war. They were so hospitable that we returned at least three times and eventually shared part of the Jesus film with them.

This contrast from the Open-Air method astonished me, and the opportunity for follow-up became a reality. It changed how I looked at ministry. I realized two significant values Muslims held. First, they are very hospitable, and second, they enjoy discussing spiritual matters. Our summer visits opened my eyes to their world—a world that did not know Christ as their Savior.

In different parts of New York, Dan and I were gaining a vision for our future ministries. Mine pointed to Central Asia, while Dan's toward Europe. He continued to discuss Sweden and his plans to establish a new Word of Life location.

Chapter Eight - Ending the time at TTU

Near the end of our time at TTU, Dan and I sought ways to spend more time together before we parted ways. A movie, "The Last Temptation of Christ," had recently come out. As we learned more about it, we agreed it was a terrible depiction of Christ's nature. We had heard that many Christians were protesting the movie, and we had no plans to watch it.

During that time, I was interning at the Highland Park Baptist Church and serving in hospital ministry under Pastor Cicero. He mentioned the protests, and I said I would be interested in joining, adding that my roommate had discussed it with me.

A few days later, in chapel, Dr. J. Don Jennings, the church pastor and university president, said how the church was against this movie and planned to protest it. Then he unexpectedly announced, "I want Dan Bubar to come forward," and as an afterthought, he mentioned my name. So, we stood, and Dan whispered to me, "Butler, what did you do?"

"Ahh, I'm not sure…"

We moved toward the front and stood below the stage while Dr. Jennings said we were organizing a protest from TTU at the Mall this Friday. "Please see them if you want to join." After this, I questioned Pastor Cicero, and he said that the rally was throughout the day, but our slot was at 8 p.m. that night. In his mind, my interest was a commitment to go.

Somehow, I had inadvertently transplanted Dan into this scenario.

"Okay, Butler. I will scope out what's happening to know what we should do."

When he returned, he said, "The 2 o'clock rally had about 60 people, and different individuals spoke about the movie."

"Well, Bubar, what are we going to do?" I inquired.

"I'm not sure, but when I left the rally, there were about 200 people there." He gulped.

"Oh, my, I didn't mean for you to get involved. By the way, I think only our roommate will join us; no one else has volunteered."

When we arrived for the 8:00 p.m. rally, approximately 800 people were present. People were everywhere throughout the Brainerd Mall parking area.[33]

There was cheering, especially right before our turn. The Pentecostal preacher cheer was: "Give me a J.... Give me an E... Give me an S... U.... S... What does that spell? ...What does that spell?"

Bubar looked at me and said, "Oh, great." Do we have to follow that?" Yet Dan, up for the challenge, spoke firmly about how it does not take a college education to know they [the movie] are blaspheming God. He riled up the crowd as a good WOL'er ought to. Skilled in his Island and youth club techniques, Dan created quite a stir, and continuous cheers came up.

Then he turned to have me come up. *Oh my, what can I say at this point*, I thought. Seeing other university students show up, in my excitement I trashed my rational proof of why the movie was off but decided instead to mention the need for young people to take a stand for God and be an example like Timothy (2 Tim. 4:12). Quoting my memory verse, I attempted to explain more why we need to live as an example because one day, shortly, we will be the leaders. Ironically, I realized it was on *that* day.

We were on the platform with the Pentecostals, Church of God, Methodists, and Baptists. We all sensed a need to take a stand against this movie. Reflecting on the event, I realize it may have been the last movie a Christian crowd protested, before the advent of accessible VCRs, online films, the handy fast-forward button, and apps like VidAngel. Today, protests often happen online.

We did not attend the rally the next day, but we were told that 6,000 people, including professional protesters, showed up.

Bundle of Stress

On one of our last nights together at TTU, Dan asked me how I thought others perceived him. He was concerned about ministering and how he came across to others. I didn't have to think long. "Dan, you are like a bundle of stress poured out on everyone around you."

He responded, "Oh…" Thinking about these words, he said, "Butler, you know what? You are right. Wow."

"Yes, a bundle of stress poured out on people."

"I know I create a lot of stress for others," he lamented.

I was thinking of the many car ventures in which Dave, his older brother, was driving while Dan verbally steered the car from the passenger seat. He would say, "Car on the right… be careful of that truck… be aware of your blind spot… don't get in a crash, Dave." It always ended with Dave being stressed out and unable to drive anymore.

Dan did everything intensely at full speed, with urgency, applying wit to ease the tension. After a while, the other person felt so stressed out they just gave Dan what he wanted or let him do it himself. In the driving situation, Dave was more than willing to give up his turn at the wheel and hand it back to Dan.

On our many trips on Interstate 81 heading back up to New York or down to Chattanooga, he had the trip mapped out in his mind. He knew how long it would take and did not want to waste time. While driving, he announced that in 20 minutes we would stop for gas and a short break. If anyone needed anything, this was *the time to get it. Buy your food and then eat it in the car.*

On one occasion, I'd had enough of *the go, go, go.*

I announced, most likely to show that he could not control me, "I will buy my lunch and eat it inside."

Bubar said, "What? No way! We have to go; time is short!"

"Okay, just see what happens."

So, I ordered my cheeseburger and sat down to eat it.

"Butler, we need to go. What are you doing? We'll be late."

I just ignored him and prepped my ketchup for my fries.

He was not happy about this, but he sat down. The others joined in also, appreciating the respite.

I knew he would not leave me there, and I figured that flexibility is a good trait for a missionary to learn.

Then I said, "Surely, life is not so serious that we can't stop for five extra minutes to eat something."

I loved Dan and his God-given ability to focus and accomplish things. He moved forward with courage and without hesitation, but we all felt his stress. Nevertheless, everyone seemed to appreciate his character and desire to please the Lord in all things. His beneficial character traits, along with his humor, helped him smooth things over with others when he realized he was being too intense.

Our Relationship

Maneuvering within each other's idiosyncrasies meant we occasionally butted heads. Dan liked to say, "Many a truth is said in jest," and over the years, we used this technique to confront each other. It was a way to convey important truths without causing undue harm. We questioned and confronted each other in this friendly, albeit not very profound, way.

Dan's brother Jonathan said, "My dad often counseled me to always listen to criticism and then take the following steps:
1. Evaluate it. Is there any truth at all to what they are saying?
2. If truth exists, take it and make the necessary adjustments.
3. If there is no truth, forget it and move on. Even a great fool can give you a nugget of truth, and truth is golden.[34]

"Son, even a fool can teach you a nugget of helpful information," his father would say.

After we finished schooling, the concept of having accountability partners entered our circles. While in seminary, I remember the care in one of Dan's letters regarding someone I was considering dating. He did not jest but dove in with his concerns. We all need friendship like this. Our teenage habit of bantering had sometimes limited a deeper relationship. Still, by the end of university, we had learned to hold each other more honestly accountable, without losing our sense of humor.

Sharing Together

Dan worked at McCallie's Boys School in the last year of university. This school's claim to fame during the late 1980s came from its alumnus, which included then President Reagan's Chief of Staff, Howard H. Baker, Jr., CNN's founder Ted Turner, as well as the Republican candidate Pat Robertson, who founded Regent University and Christian Broadcasting Network.[35]

Dan sat at a desk for about four hours as the night librarian, ensuring that each student entered and signed in to record their study hours. One student who stood out to him was someone he thought might be Ted Turner's son. Dan tried to engage him in conversation but with little success.[36]

The library job was a piece of cake for Dan, and he enjoyed interacting with the students. Notably, Dan engaged in a spiritual conversation with a man named Dana. Dan shared the gospel with him and said he was pretty open. Because Dan had enough credits, he planned to finish TTU a semester early. So, late in the fall, he introduced me to the head librarian to take his place. Based on his recommendation and the fact that I had also worked a semester at the TTU library, the switch became an easy choice for them.

Dan mentioned that Dana was open to the gospel, and we prayed for him to come to know the Lord. So, when I took the desk job there, I got to know him. He seemed to possess a natural intellect and was open to discussing spiritual matters. One day, he showed me an occult book about demons. Out of concern for him, I mentioned that he should be careful, as this type of stuff could lead him down the wrong path.

I did not realize Dana's intent in showing me this book.

I arrived at the library one evening for work before Spring Break. The head librarian lady called me in and showed me a letter written to the editor of the local *Chattanooga Times*. The letter was from a student at the McCallie's Boys School. The student said he'd shown a staff member at the library a *book that did not favor the staff's religious beliefs*. The staff member, attending TTU and studying religion, critiqued the book and attempted to limit his freedom of choice. Then, he described how important his personal liberties and choices were.

She asked me, *Did you say these things?* I replied honestly that I had seen the book and had given a word of caution, but the writer had exaggerated. She suspected so, but warned me to be careful about what I said to students while working at McCallie. As I surveyed the other letters, there were a few from the school, and it became apparent that an English class had assigned the task of writing a letter to the paper's editor.

Later, Dana admitted that he'd elaborated just a bit, and it was a good laugh for him. Yet, as a future minister overseas, I needed to understand my audience and relate to them accordingly, starting with Chattanooga. The art of Apologetics is a rocky road when others seek to find fault. After this incident, I thought twice before saying something in this context.

Dan helped with provisions so I could graduate debt-free. Once this job started, I was working approximately 55 hours a week: 15 hours at a restaurant on weekends, 20 hours as a night librarian, and 20 hours as a music building monitor at TTU. Forty hours allowed me to study and do extra reading. Wow, the Lord provided 40 paid hours a week to sit at desks and monitor sign-in sheets till the buildings were closed for the night.

Dan and Honey

In the final days before our graduation ceremony, Dan returned to the dorm. When we woke up, Dan started the kettle to make his tea, and I headed down the hall to the shower.

Then, as I walked back to the end room on the third floor, I could smell the black tea, with a hint of honey, in the air. The hotpot had just turned off, and Dan sat at his desk, stirring in his honey. As I entered, he said, *"My son, eat thou honey, because it is good; and the honeycomb, which is sweet to thy taste"* (Proverbs 24:13, KJV). Dan was obsessed with honey and proverbs about honey. As a person of ritual, he quoted a honey proverb possibly every time he stirred his honey into his tea.

"It smells good. Can I have a cup?" I asked. Then, with our cups in hand, we continued our quiet time, reading the word.

Dan believed in the life-giving properties of honey and enjoyed its sweetness. Likewise, he was a Proverb Expositor, sharing different ones whenever possible.

He desired not just to add honey to his tea but to add wisdom to his life. If I am not mistaken, he continued, *"So shall the knowledge of wisdom be unto thy soul: when thou hast found it, then there shall be a reward, and thy expectation shall not be cut off"* (Proverbs 24:14). For Dan, morning tea and finding treasure in God's word were an inseparable pair.

I recall being discouraged about memorizing verses. I asked Dan about it, and he said Proverbs is a good book for ministry, noting that it is handy for counseling. He had memorized multiple verses from Proverbs to better relate to others.

"It is not good to eat much honey; so for men to search their own glory is not glory" (Proverbs 25:27 KJV). He quoted this not to put too much honey in his tea but also as a reminder not to seek self-glory. He admired how his dad modeled this truth.

Paul Bubar founded WOL Clubs, which later went into the hands of Mike Calhoun. He directed the Island for a few years but then handed this over to others who developed the program. Dan's father took over the overseas department and established a structure that promoted growth. Yet his dad did not seek glory or complain about any loss of his ministry "babies." Dan longed to imitate his dad's example and honor the Lord.

Years after that morning with the tea, I was reminded of Dan's pet verses. One of the leading believers in our house church in Central Asia shared that, as a child, he had a fondness for honey. One day, however, he ate so much that he became sick. After this, he never ate honey again, even in old age. He could have benefited from a Proverbs scholar like Dan during his childhood.

Call to DO IT

At the end of 1988, while studying in our university dorm, out of the blue, Dan said, *"Faithful is He that calleth you, who also will DO IT.* First Thessalonians 5:24. We must be faithful to what God wants us to do. What will you do?"

"That reminds me of our missions conference at the BI in '85: *Say it, don't delay it, just do it.* A great challenge that now sounds like this year's new Nike theme," I said.

"God works through young people, and I want to work with the European youth. Bollback went to the jungles of Brazil, and Sophie Muller went to the Amazon. Our generation must go behind the Iron Curtain, and the coming winds of change connect to the Soviet Union region."

"How do you know?" I asked.

"Look at our WOL missionaries Chuck Kosman and Bob Parschauer. They have already visited the Soviet Union and said great opportunities exist. Our generation needs to explore these new opportunities."

"Well, my time in Bangladesh last year showed me one thing: a person will be doing a lot of teaching on the mission field. My mission degree has prepared me to be a mission representative, but not to teach. I need to get a master's degree in teaching."

Bubar responded, "Butler, now is the time to go. Europe is falling apart. I already know the WOL program. I can do clubs, camps, and discipleship now. I see no seminary in my future. I've lived WOL all my life and am now ready to do it. I'm ready to go and learn the language."

I pleaded, "Are you sure? I can't talk you into going to the Muslim or Hindu world? They are the least-reached. Europe has had the gospel for years and already has many churches, but many places in Asia have none." I didn't want our paths to separate, finally.

He responded, "The world's youth await, and they need the gospel. They are the ones who will bring the gospel to the least-reached."

"Bubar, you are the epitome of Word of Life."

How would we know where to go? Knowledge about a place can open the heart's door to an interest. Praying about our interests led both of us to act. We trusted Christ for insight and direction. My interest started with Jews and then Muslims. The former Soviet Union and Eastern Europe were the open doors of our generation, and the Persian connection kept coming into my path. Eventually, knowing that God had placed these circumstances in my way to guide me, I followed this path.

In considering God's will, a strong sense of generational obligation tugged at my heart. God is always at work among the nations, revealing new opportunities to each generation. For us, Eastern Europe and the Soviet Union centered our thoughts. I had noticed throughout my life that no missionary I had heard of had been sent to Syria, but a new opportunity arose after the outbreak of war in 2011. For the first time, ministers in Lebanon, Türkiye, and Iraq had a chance to reach those who had fled. It was as if God had arranged or allowed them to flee so they could hear the gospel. We must identify the global opportunities that lie before us and, as a church, move in that new direction.

I recall at TTU, sitting in a seminar taught by the Friends of Israel and feeling real peace about working with Jewish people — their culture so close to the Bible. Yet the stats bothered me. During those days, few missions aimed to reach out to Muslims, and Chattanooga had a few Jewish mission organizations located there. Also, the number of Jews in the world compared to the number of Muslims approached an imbalance I could not ignore. These statistics spoke to me.

With this tension in my heart, I wrote, "Where the Lord leads, I don't know, but I know He will lead. He is able to do above all that I ask or even think. This is exciting to know."[37]

When we thought about ministry, my burden was for the least-reached, and Dan's was for youth. Later, I read about a man who complained to Mother Teresa about not having the time to serve the lepers he worked with. He said, "I am not called to do all these extra things but to work with lepers."

Mother Teresa responded, "You are not called to lepers but to Jesus." We could rejoice in our differences, and the bottom line was this: We wanted to serve Jesus wherever he led us.

Graduation and Beyond

Everyone was placed alphabetically during graduation, which meant we got to sit together: Daniel, David Bubar, and me. For years, Dave was located across the hallway from us, and, like his brother, he studied a lot. On that day, all three of us graduated with the class of 1989.

At that point, we would move in different directions. Dan and Dave drove back to New York. Dan was already making plans to move overseas, but the Lord had shown me how ill-prepared I was for ministry overseas. I had spent the summer of 1988 in Bangladesh and realized I needed to learn how to teach. So while Dan was heading to Europe, I was heading to Dallas Theological Seminary to pursue studies in Christian Education. He already had a life of Christian education and was steeped in the philosophy and scope of Word of Life. His training prepared him for the task ahead, and his drive would produce further fruitfulness. My life did not have the same background, nor was I heading into a set program like Word of Life. However, we both were thrilled to graduate and move on to the next chapter. With the scholarships and years of work the Lord provided, we were able to graduate debt-free.

While the degree invited us to our next steps, it also marked an end. We realized our paths would cross sparingly from that point on.

Chapter Nine - Dan's Calling

Recalling our debate on church planting, we knew that God put different desires into our heart. After graduation, the daily reality of missions set in.

Praying for a Future Location

In May 1989, immediately after graduation, Dan attended Missionary Training to join WOL officially. Plans concerning Hungary were progressing quite quickly, but Dan was still focused on Sweden. His appointment to Sweden was likely the first for WOL, and he did not have a large team. I think he was the only one heading that way at that point.

How does one determine the location or country where God's will is? The needs are plentiful everywhere, but is there a specific call to a country? The first step in discerning God's will is to pray. Pray for his direction and guidance. Dan did this and prayed for his future, which tended to focus on Europe. He assessed his family background and the opportunities that lay before him. He wanted to step out on faith and, ideally, to start something new.

On his mother's side, the Swanson family was of 100% Swedish descent, making this a fitting place for him to start a ministry. It would be like going home. Also, during those days, WOL was considering ministry there. I heard from Dan, however, that starting there had a few bumps because Sweden had another group called Word of Life. Although

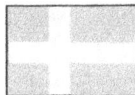

DANIEL BUBAR
Word of Life Sweden

"Faithful is He that calleth you, who also will DO IT."
I Thess. 5:24

Dan's first prayer card

Word of Life Fellowship (the official name of the organization here) had already registered its trademark, another group began operating a church in 1983 under the same name. Since then, they have planted a few churches, and this local group has become a mega-church. Ultimately, I think WOL Fellowship conceded to not entering this country. This situation made Dan's future unsure, and he lamented to me during our conversations during this time.

The Call to Join Bubar

In April, a month before our graduation, Dan called me at TTU from New York.[38]

"Hey, I'm going to Hungary with a new team. I won't be going to Sweden after all."

"Wow, that's great. Why the change of plans?" I asked.

"We are the generation to walk into this new open door. My dad has been there numerous times, and unbelievable opportunities exist."

"Will you have a team there?" I asked.

"There is a small team, and now that Hungary is on the verge of change, we need to move quickly and act. Do you know we have gained permission to form a camp at a castle there?"

The opening of this land to WOL was a miracle in itself. Dan's dad labored against forces that did not want this ministry there. WOL wrote, "The tension between Paul's dream and the Hungarian status quo was intense. The Hungarian Minister of Churches accused Paul of being a CIA agent and informed him he was unwelcome in Hungary. Hungarians told him his mission was impossible and warned him to leave before it was too late. One church leader met Paul in a hotel lobby and said, 'You must leave and cannot come back.' The very existence of Word of Life Hungary is as much a testament to Paul's humility, firm faith, and hopeful good humor as it is to the Lord's divine provision, timing, and awesome power over the mortal world."[39] I sensed something special was taking place, and I knew Dan was meant to go there.

Dan continued, "Butler, I want you to join me on this team. This is a new open door, and we need you there."

"You know my calling, Bubar; my prayers are with you," I said, feeling honored that he had asked me to work with him. God had been showing me other open doors. I had read that 51 million Muslims lived in the Soviet Union. Still, only two Central Asian churches exist among them (this stat did not consider the multiple Russian-speaking churches in the area, which I later learned). I gave Dan a summary of these ideas and then continued, "I need to study teaching, and Dallas Theological Seminary has accepted me."

That night, I wrote: *"I know Dan wants me full-time, but I can't — I know it would not be God's will. Often, I've thought about being single-minded and keep [going] ahead on with Muslims" (April 22, 1989).*

Ken Dady's words related to my tension: "Circumstances never made a man; God makes a man and then works out circumstances later."

It Was Harry's Idea

In the historical write-up by Paul Bubar, *Not by Chance*, the Lord used the words of the co-founder of Word of Life, Harry Bollback, to prompt Dan's call. Harry said, "Your son, Dan, must come to Hungary and minister. This is the field for him. Call Dan today"[40] (April 1989). It was clear the Holy Spirit was at work.

Strangely, all the great things that happened and are still happening at Word of Life are two-tiered. One is the public excitement about what the founders of Word of Life, such as Jack Wyrtzen and Harry Bollback, along with directors like George Theis and Joe Jordan, have accomplished. We hear their stories of faith and their adventures in evangelism. They are the spiritual "giants in the land."

The other tier is steps of obedience of everyday believers sharing and ministering on the multiple programs of Word of Life. Previously, the simple step of faith in buying the Island, the Inn (Lodge), and the many other properties worldwide initiated opportunity. The addition of countries worldwide opened the door to expansion and growth. Or, in Dan's case, a simple gesture of confidence in a young man.

I recall Harry Bollback's repeated sermon about *Feeding the 5,000,* which I never grew tired of hearing: "Little becomes much when God is in it!" — he would say. That statement alone sums up the great God we have. He can use each of us and, with the little we offer, multiply it to become much.

J. Oswald Sanders said, "The man of vision is willing to take fresh steps of faith when there is only a seeming void beneath."

God had arranged circumstances to lead Dan to the brink of this void, but by then, Dan's foot was bold, and he readily took that step of faith.

Pre-Field Ministry

Pre-field ministry is when a missionary shares their vision with churches and individuals. They also minister in whatever way the church needs them to. This period is often referred to as deputation or support raising. It can be difficult, embarrassing, and fun, but it is always faith-building. During September and October 1989, Dan traveled to 13 churches. One day, after driving 6 hours, he arrived at his destination too early and took the opportunity to write me a letter.

From the church parking lot, he wrote:

"So far, I've got 22% $660 a mo. in, and this is all from individuals. One lady just took me on for $200 a mo. I've never met her, but she used to date my Dad's roommate when he went to Barrington. When she heard about me going to Hungary, she had to have a 'small part' in it. At least four of the churches that I've been to have 'promised' support, so actually, I'm probably somewhere around 30%. Boy, am I pretty zipped. So far, I've traveled around 1,200 [miles] a week or more" (Oct 14, 1989).

God calls individuals — Abraham, Hagar, Moses, Aaron, Samuel, Hannah, Isaiah, Jeremiah, and many more. These men and women were conscious that God called them and then persuaded them to act to fulfill his will. As they obeyed each step of the way, the Lord continued to work out the plan he had for them in a unique way.

Each calling was unique. God guided each person through training situations that eventually led to a passion. Though not all callings are the same, the source of them is. *"And no one takes this honor for himself, but only when called by God, just as Aaron was" (Heb. 5:4).* Although we may have been honored by the churches that supported us, God's sacred desire cannot be taken as a personal honor. One's calling is an extension of God's heart. When we are called, we are witnessing and experiencing his nature, not our own.

I remember going on Spring Break to New Hampshire with our WOLBI roommate, Dick Bodie, and sitting with a minister of Navigators at McDonald's. The focus that day was on Luke 9:23, *"And he said to all, 'If anyone would come after me, let him deny himself and take up his cross daily and follow me.' "* The teacher stressed that denying oneself means disregarding one's personal interests. That lesson has stayed with me since — a daily disregard for individual choices. Motives checked and a daily taking up of the cross. What did I consider a matter of personal interest? I did not sense that Dan had any worldly personal interest, as he was deeply immersed in WOL focus.

However, at times, my heart leaned toward personal benefit. My grandpa was an accountant for the municipal government in Richmondville, NY. As a child, I thought working with money could make me rich. Later, my enjoyment of baking led me to the culinary world. Would Johnson & Wales or Culinary Institute of America be an option? I could have my own restaurant or bakery. What could be better than getting up early and finishing all one's work by 3 pm? I would have the rest of the day for myself and my life. The bakery atmosphere at Word of Life Inn gave me a hunger for something more. Yet was my calling into a spiritual ministry or to an occupation?

Luke 9:23 drove me to consider my motives. *Am I regarding my own interests? Lord, when I follow you, what does this mean?* Regarding working with Dan in WOL, I sensed that it would be enjoyable and aligned with my interests, but God was asking me to set aside my personal desires and follow an unfamiliar path. God asked Dan the same, yet it led to a different place.

His dad summarized Dan's call: "For more than twenty years, Dan watched and observed how everything was done. He studied the Word of Life camp program and dreamed of one day being able to run a Word of Life Camp."[41]

Calling and Dating

Dan also wrote on Oct. 14, 1989, *"So far, there are no women in my life. I'm too busy, but that's nothing new. I got a letter yesterday from Millie Bollback and Ken Buxbaum. They want me to write Faith H. and get reacquainted, but I can't remember when we were ever acquainted to begin with."* This is humorous; she worked with us at the Inn, and I even corresponded with her sometimes. But knowing Faith, this was not her doing; instead, these matchmakers were zealous about directing Dan toward a spiritually-minded lady. Nevertheless, he remained focused on God's timing, even if it meant going to the field single.

In our correspondence, he mentioned some personal prayer requests, and then a few months later, on Jan. 30, 1990, he said,

"My support is coming in really well. I'm up to 70%, but I still need 30% plus $6,600 for a sound system by May 3. I know the Lord will send it in."

"I'm really busy in meetings. I've never spoken more in my life."

"I really don't mind deputation. Actually, it's rather exciting. It sure beats selling grave lots."

Nevertheless, he prayed, as he said, with one eye open. He hoped God would give him a spouse before the departure date. Either way, he would go, and the Lord would lead.

Concerning this theme, I quote his letters:

"I've managed to strike up a nice relationship with a fine young lady. I told you a little about her when you called around Christmas. Well, Butler, you'll never believe it, but she still likes me. I leave for Hungary around May 3, though, and that could definitely hurt our relationship if I let it" (Jan. 30, 1990).

He planned to visit her in Indiana in March of 1990. He said, *"Well, Jeff, to sum up, my life for the last two mo.s would be to say Tera — Deputation — Christmas — Tera — Deputation — Hungary — Tera — Deputation. Actually, it has been pretty exciting"* (Jan. 30, 1990).

"I'm still writing to Tera, but I know that the time and distance have hurt our relationship. She's really slowed down things quite a bit, and maybe, when I go home in August, she'll ditch me for good. Maybe not. She's young and needs lots of time, so things are 'wait and see' right now. If you think about it pray for this situation. I've had to just leave it all in the Lord's hands and trust Him with the outcome. I can't let it get in the way of ministry this summer. I refuse to" (July 12, 1990).

His words describe a driven man heading to Hungary, where he realizes his loneliness.

One woman I met during the summer Muslim outreach training said that relationships *are often like lampposts*. They provide us with some guidance to move on to the next step. Christian dating requires much wisdom, and ending any relationship without using or harming the other involves care. At this point, we both wanted more than a lamppost. We kept praying with one eye open.

His pastor, Roger Ellison, said, "Dan was single and alone but ready to do what God called him to do, whether anybody else did or not."

A key point in my TTU experience came from my Missions professor, Mickey Johnson, who often discussed one's call to missions. He said his wife was not necessarily called to missions but was called to him. At first, this concept did not sit right with me because I felt both ought to be called to the work. However, I wish I had asked him why he said this. He did not mean that God cannot call women to missions, and his statement most likely explained a nuance between his wife's and his calling. But it made me think.

Can a person be called to another person? A critical discussion during the 1980s in Christian universities was how to define God's will. Was God's will a dot or a broad area? Garry Friesen's book, *Decision Making and the Will of God*, highlighted this discussion. As singles, we all thought, "Where is my dot?" Is my wife to be a dot or one of many possible options? The discussion served as a means to illustrate how God's will operates. He guides and sets up circumstances to teach us what specific things He may have in mind for us.

While dating, I never bought into the *dot* theory that there is only one person for me out there. I reasoned that if a person got married and then claimed they had not found their dot, they could later conclude that they were mistaken and had actually missed their dot. If I miss my dot, then what? What if I marry the wrong dot? The consequences of this logic did not seem to bode commitment. Instead, I strongly felt that once God brought my wife and me together in marriage, she was my dot; there was no other for me.

Professor Johnson's offhand comment that his wife was called to him settled into the middle of the debate on God's will for the mission field. Did God call Dan to WOL? Yes! He considered Sweden, and was this the place for him? He could have gone there, but in discerning God's will for himself, the doors to Sweden closed while the door to Hungary swung wide open. For him, which country to focus on became an easy switch. However, the dating aspect still saturated our minds and prayers.

God's Further Provisions

While Dan trusted in finding his support to go overseas, my test came when I entered Dallas Theological Seminary. My first year was over, and I needed to earn more money to cover my seminary costs. Looking at the job board, I saw that a couple was seeking a seminary student to live with them and care for their lawn, house, pool, and, occasionally, their dogs. The advertisement stated that it offered free room and board. Undoubtedly, many would seek this incredible opportunity. I quickly called, and they invited me over. After a meal together, they invited me to move in. This enabled me to work and pay only for school and vehicle costs. This was enough, so my room and board for the next two and a half years were taken care of. Strangely enough, the couple said I was the only one answering the advertisement. I knew God had meant it for me.

During my last semester in the Seminary, I had to make a choice. I wanted to graduate in the spring but did not have enough money to pay for the next semester. So I took out a loan, figuring a semester of work would be enough time to pay it off. During that time, my car problems multiplied. I had to put to rest the old car my dad had given me and buy a very cheap car. "Lemon," as a friend and I called it, was a yellow Rabbit with a taste for new parts. This gracious friend also helped me install the parts to avoid labor costs.

In the end, Lemon died in a church parking lot, billowing smoke and fire from the battery that someone gave me but installed incorrectly.

However, I continued to see how God provided in the craziest ways through various circumstances and people. After Lemon, the Lord provided a Chevy Cavalier convertible to buy. A family had taken the car away from their teen daughter when she was given a DWI. These friends were willing to sell it for a minimal amount rather than let it sit in their driveway, which meant I would eventually use this convertible during pre-field ministry. I do not recommend this method, but the Lord demonstrated his supply.

I would drive the car to a church to meet the pastor or a deacon. Upon seeing the convertible blue sports car, they would usually ask, "How did you come to drive a convertible?" I was then able to share the story of God's provision after my car burned up in Dallas.

As I mentioned, debt is one reason people do not go overseas. My mission organization's policy at the time was that one must be debt-free before leaving for the mission field. I had a remaining debt of $3,500 from the loan I'd taken out, and my only asset was the car.

The week before I left, I put a "for sale" sign on the car and parked it on the edge of my mom's property. I was pretty busy preparing to leave and didn't have time to meet with potential buyers. So, I negotiated with my brother to sell it on my behalf. The deal was that anything over $3,500 was his. Eventually, one of his friends bought the convertible for $ 3,550, and he earned $50.

I put the money in the bank and wrote the check. On the day I was heading to the airport to go overseas for the first time, I stopped by the post office and dropped off a check for $ 3,500 to pay off my remaining debt. The Lord had provided once again, enabling me to be debt-free just in time. Praise the Lord for his provisions. Though he often uses trials that require initiative and creativity, when he calls, he also provides.

Philosophy on Finances

Dan loved the book of Proverbs, and so often, when we had a challenge, it was the first place we would look. We discovered that Proverbs 30 encapsulated our philosophy on finances.

Proverbs 30:7-9 says:

[7] *Two things have I required of thee; deny me them not before I die:* [8] *Remove far from me vanity and lies: give me neither poverty nor riches; feed me with food convenient for me:* [9] *Lest I be full, and deny thee, and say, Who is the LORD? or lest I be poor, and steal, and take the name of my God in vain" (KJV).*

The two key factors are striking a balance between having enough and understanding one's needs. Keeping needs and wants within perspective so as not to covet or do unjustly. Like the wise man Agur, who penned these inspired words, I did not want to be in such a state of want that temptation would come in how money was spent or received. Submitting work-related expenses became a regular task as a worker, and I often relied on reimbursement. Theoretically, one could easily fudge the amount or add other expenses, but the standard of integrity demanded otherwise. Another biblical challenge is to find contentment in what the Lord provides (Hebrews 13:5). Since He supplies all our needs (Phil. 4:19), we can trust that it is enough, becoming wise stewards of whatever He gives.

In light of Proverbs 30:7-9, I developed a philosophy for approaching finances. These were the days before books like Friend Raising came out. For us, God calls, and he supplies. He will do it.

We both realized that being a missionary was about raising awareness, not money. We taught about mission-related topics, endeavoring *to inspire others to respond in whatever way God was calling them.*

With my Christian Education background at Dallas, I was motivated to focus more on educating others rather than asking for support.So, early on, an emphasis on the need in ministry while teaching something new about the people, culture, or situation. Questions arose about the opportunity, which would enable one to provide some details about the place or people.

I created and adapted games for use in my teaching with both adults and children. Like Dan, I enjoyed the experience and trusting God to relieve our burdens. Another game was called Missions Outburst, which focused on questions about Muslims.

For children, the game "Where in the World is Carmen Missionary?" allowed kids to choose between three countries related to the ministry, each represented by a different spot in the room. After asking a question, participants stood near the country that fit the description, and I encouraged them to explain their choice. This way, each question became an opportunity to teach about missions.

Finances became a minor consideration, while teaching became the focus. Based on Dan's letters and my own experience, I believe *God provides where you least expect it.* Over the years, I have seen this. Sometimes, my expectations did not reflect my faith in God. Instead, they were based on my logic.

Once, I was sure a church would support the ministry, but then I ended up with an individual who had supported the work for decades but not the church. God was constantly surprising me with unexpected donors, and each time, I was amazed at his provision.

Before I left Dallas, I presented in one of the Sunday School classes at the church that Ross Perot attended. Now, Ross Perot had made a semi-successful independent run for the Presidency of the US and was a well-known billionaire. Though he was not in the class, other millionaires were. I thought that surely someone would throw a few thousand my way after this presentation. Well, my live-in family, who had invited me, helped out a bit for a year, but no one else did from this group. On the other hand, one woman on the seminary staff gave up her daily coffee on the way to work to support the ministry.

Pre-field ministry is a faith-stretching time, and every worker can give many examples of God's creative provision.

While I was finishing up my time in Dallas and preparing for my pre-field ministry to head overseas, Dan was serving full-time in Hungary.

118

Chapter Ten - Initial Years in Hungary

"Today is the first day of the rest of your life, so make it a masterpiece" ~Dr. Clarence Diden (July 6, 1982, WOL Inn).

Dan wanted to invest his life in a new ministry with WOL. Jack Wyrtzen had started something new, just as his Dan's dad had. As a young pastor, his dad met Jack, and together, they dreamed of how to reach young people. Mr. Bubar loved to reach out to non-Christians and also enjoyed discipling young people. He envisioned a youth program incorporating Bible reading, memorization, and Christian service. So Dan grew up while WOL was only a generation old, and the desire to tread new ground seemed to rub off on him. In many ways, Dan's and mine were identical callings. We aspired to create a new foundation that would spark a fresh beginning, all while honoring the divine design set forth by God (Romans 15:20).

A call is a sense of doing God's will for a particular purpose. Sometimes, it starts with just meeting a need. It is a realization that God is leading and enabling one to do a specific task.

Dan did not just work for Word of Life; he had been living and breathing WOL his entire life, as God had prepared him for a specific calling. When he recognized the need to reach Eastern European youth, his passion perfectly aligned with this new mission. Everything he aspired to accomplish was encapsulated in this endeavor.

The call became a necessity and an obligation—almost an obsession with doing WOL in Hungary. No other organization existed in his mind; all he knew and what shaped him was the organization his parents served in. He wanted to live in a new setting, build a new foundation, and see what God had in store for him in Hungary.

"One thing I will miss is the Island this summer, but on the other hand, maybe I'll be so busy in Hungary that I won't have time to notice. The camp property is really something. Tremendous possibilities. The latest news is that Chris Miller[42] and Dave James[43] are planning on going over in Sept of '91 to start the B.I. in Hungary. Can you imagine that? What a team!" (Jan. 30, 1990).

The property in Hungary was a castle located in the center of a village, intimately connected to the community. It would provide a social identity and a secure place to meet for ministry. Some debate that a building is unnecessary, but for WOL Hungary, it was crucial to maintaining the vision and heartbeat of Word of Life ministries. God always provides what we need, and he graciously gave this location to the ministry.

Dan sent me a picture of the Dedication Day on May 19-20, 1990. On the back of the photograph, he said, *"Real enthusiasm here for this ministry, close to 1000 in attendance."*

Dan just stepped into the lives of the team of ministers, pastors, and youth leaders who were already quite active in their service. The WOL Hungary program gave a new initiative, vision, and empowerment to see this generation of youth come to the Lord.

"Hungary camp is really cranking. We are averaging around 65 campers a week. We've got some great counselors. The staff is working very hard on renovations. Things are busy. At the end of the 3rd week out of 7, over 70 young people have trusted Christ. It's unbelievable the way people are turning to Christ" (Dan's letter, July 12, 1990).

The WOL circle presented the story of Hungary as a miracle, but that was not Dan's motivation for going. When I read Paul Bubar's book *Not by Chance,* I realized that Hungary was a field ripe for harvest. Politically, the country resisted communism in 1955, and the churches remained steadfast in their commitment to the gospel despite significant political pressure. Ironically, WOL Hungary began its work in 1990, a full year before the Soviet troops exited the country in June 1991. Due to the political conditions affecting the churches, their freedoms were quite limited at that time. WOL registered outside of the Ministry of Religion, which allowed them extra freedoms to operate.

Street meetings

"Last Saturday [July 7], I went into Budapest with the Jr. Team Word of Life Quartet, and we had a street meeting. Hundreds (literally) stopped to listen, and we invited those interested in accepting Christ to take a tract. After an hour, our box of tracts was empty. The crowd was so big that the police came to break it up. They said they were afraid of pickpocketing" (July 12, 1990).

He knew that ministry was challenging and that many barriers would get in the way, yet he trusted God and was tenacious in pursuing His will.

121

Dan kept himself busy. In a letter to me on September 1991, he wrote, *"Right now I'm burnt tired—8 months straight and hard with no break except a day off weekly. I asked for it, and I would [not] want to be doing anything else. My vacation comes in 2 weeks."* He said the first three months were the hardest, but he was okay because he trusted he was where God wanted him.

Laughably, Dan was too busy to learn to cook or do his laundry. Perhaps those things had fallen off his list of priorities, but he conveniently dropped in near his teammates' mealtime to see what was cooking. Or, sometimes, he would use this creative approach:

"Rich, I'm standing outside Pizza Hut and wondering what to do. Should I go in, or are there better options?"

His teammate, Rich Hood, knew what Dan meant. "Dan, come on over. We are about to eat supper." This was a common occurrence for him.

His father described it this way, *"In Budapest, he could not cook. All he could cook was eggs. He had a way in showing up during meal times. He had a reputation for that... He called Olga Nini, 'This is Dan, I am at a payphone at a McDonalds, ahh… What should I do?'"*

Ministry in 1991

Listen to Dan's words about serving in Hungary.

"The ministry here is exploding out our ears — all groups included close to 1700 guests or more at the camp this summer. Our second [summer]" (Sept. 1991).

"Things are going well over here. I'd be lying to say it's easy and that sometimes I don't wonder to myself by asking, 'What have I gotten myself into here?' Every day and month gets easier as I learn the culture. The first 3 months were the hardest. The biggest thing, I guess, is maintaining a proper attitude when it's easier not to.

Life can be extremely frustrating at times. You wait in lines for everything here, and you know how I love to wait in lines. Ha-ha!! But I can make it because I know I'm where God wants me, and that's all that matters anyway. Life can also be really rewarding here, too, as people have open and sensitive hearts to sin and to Christ. They are more than happy to talk with you always. Life has a much slower pace than in America. This is something I'm really coming to enjoy. Sure, there's no telephone, but then again, there's no phone, to answer all the time, to call everyone. People read more books here because there's no cable T.V. and few VCRs. All this will change in the next 5-10 years, though" (Sept. 1991).

"Believe it, Jeff, last Saturday we did our first WOL Saturday in a local church — it turned out very similar to those I was involved with on the weekends in Chattanooga. A Pizza Bash — Jelopi [Jalopy] Raid. We doubled our attendance from 40-80 with unsaved. Eric Murphy preached, and 26 came to Christ. Our counselors spent one hour with them afterward (10 counselors were at camp this summer) and would have gone longer had the pizza not been ready" (Oct. 17, 1991).

When we talked, Dan spoke highly of national leaders and planned events with them. He wrote, *"It's exciting for me to see WOL become that much more nationalized last weekend"* (Oct 17, 1991). Dan's agenda was to run a program and incarnate himself in Hungarian society to share the light of his Savior. Moreover, there was a need to nationalize the ministry so that Hungarians could lead it.

"It's children's week here at Tóalmás and my right arm — Ban Laslo is back and taking some of the load off, so I can catch my breath and write you back."

"I think back often on how God guided me here and the people he used in my life along the way. You were a big player. You were and still are an influencer on me and a very good friend. Know that you will always be a friend. It's good to know that kind of thing" (Oct. 17, 1991).

He stretched himself to cast off his Western ways and adopted Eastern European ones as much as possible.

Partnering with other groups

I knew of an ABWE missionary who went to Budapest, and I asked Dan about how they would work together. Both groups had the intention of starting a Bible School, and I wondered how much collaboration existed initially. I thought getting this off the ground would require a lot of effort, so I asked about the initial level of collaboration.

He responded, *"Yes, I see Nester (ABWE missionary) at least once every two weeks. They haven't got their school going yet, and neither have we, but I'm sure that we will work together, perhaps in the exchange of teachers, but this is two years down the road. We have a luncheon planned here at Tóalmás on June 2 for all the* boards working in Hungary. You know that we can't work hand in hand with everyone, but with many of them. It also helps to get together to encourage one another and to exchange information" *(April 1992).* It is a wise course of action to realize one is not the only ministry in the area—the many new works there had the advantage of building on existing networks.

He signed his letter with Phil. 3:14, *"I press toward the mark for the prize of the high calling of God in Christ Jesus. His for Hungary."*

I know he was pressing on with as much enthusiasm as possible, unaware of his shortness of time.

Spring 1992

Dan summarized his spring: *"We have just started what will be the month in which the largest number of campers will come to Tóalmás, April '92. Everyone is counting down the hours until Euro-Youth and wondering if all the work will be done in time... Every morning at breakfast devotions, we have been praying that the Lord would do something in the hearts of those coming. April 16th is the day when over 700 campers will arrive from all over Europe, and at about 2 o'clock in the afternoon, the first service will begin, your time. If you think about it, pray for us, then that the Lord would especially use His Word as it goes forth to minister in the lives of the young people that will be there"* (April 1992).

His summer camp picture was on the Hungarian brochure's second page. He sent me one (now lost) and said, *"Recognize the weird-looking guy on the second page of the brochure? I wouldn't tell anyone if I did"* (April 1992).

Fall, 1992

Hear Dan's impression of the spiritual climate of the day: *"Last Friday, October 23 [1992] was the 36th anniversary of the 1956 revolution. I was taking part in a Baptist youth conference in Kiskoros with around 700 young people. The theme of the conference was 'Vigazzatok, hogy eltek' (Be careful how you live, Ephesians 5:15). It was aimed at warning the young people against the many false teachings that have swept into Hungary in the last year, especially the Hary Krishna, Mormons and the signs and wonders evangelist as well. It was a thrill to be one of the seminar speakers and to meet with young people that really have a desire to live for the Lord.*

"The next day I was in Budapest for a meeting regarding the opening of the CBMC (Christian Businessmen's Association) Upon arriving home, I caught the evening news broadcast, I saw that while I was in Kiskoros, they were having "1956 Revolution celebration in Budapest." It was a cold night with a little rain and so the crowd was smaller than the usual to hear the President, Gonz Arpad, give his annual address. It wasn't too cold to keep away a group of misguided, skin-headed young people, though, and they made such a commotion with their shouting insults that the President was shocked and visibly concerned for his safety. Rather than calling in the police and making a riot out of the whole scene, the old gentleman, who was imprisoned [under the communist rule] for his stand for freedom, simply went home that evening without making a speech. Later, I found out that the Alex Konya family was on the front row that night and eye-witnessed the whole commotion" (Oct. 28, 1992).*

He continues, *"No question about it, we are in a spiritual conflict here. On one side, Christians are being lured into false teaching, and on the other, the world, the flesh, and the devil are advancing with full force on the young. Praise the Lord that He is working in the midst of all of this. At the Youth Conference, I met a young man who was saved at the camp this year. He said that three years ago, his oldest sister was saved; last year, his younger sister, and this summer, he also received Christ. He asked me when the Bible Institute would be started, because he wants to go. The Lord is calling out a people for His name, and it's great to be a part of that kind of work"* (Oct. 28, 1992).

He also mentions that, near this time, *"There are some real tensions building here as well, as you have read, but comparatively speaking, Hungary is the least 'sick' amongst the eastern countries."*

"Super Pretzel Loves You!! But you probably haven't gotten any letters from him for a while. Sorry, buddy, but you know my skills are in the area of mass mailings instead of personal letters, and even in that area they are lacking. In spite of all this my support hasn't drop[ped] off completely. I want a list of where you will be from Jan. to March. I am coming home (Schroon Lake) for a real brief furlough on Dec. 19 and then heading back on the 5th of April.

I do hope to catch up with you when I'm in the States. I'll be traveling quite a bit, and so if I know your schedule, I can probably see you sometime. Hope all is well with you and I'm proud of you. Keep on for the Lord" (Oct. 28, 1992).

Chapter Eleven - Finding a Bride at the BI

After graduating from DTS, I joined Christar and planned to head to the Middle East to work with Persian speakers. After working in Dallas during the fall and completing pre-field ministry there, I moved back to New York.

Dan ended his letter dated October 28, 1992, with "See you at Christmas?" I was excited to begin my journey overseas, and seeing Bubar again was a bonus. He came home for Christmas to be with family. I returned to conduct pre-field ministry near my hometown and at Perth Bible Church.

After many experiences apart, we were both excited to finally have the opportunity to meet up in person. The WOLBI missions conference in January 1993 marked a key event that significantly influenced my life.

Bubar Bed & Breakfast

Being with Dan again was an incredible thrill after not seeing each other for a few years. We had just spent three years in different places: me in Dallas and him in Hungary. He still wore his smirking smile and remained serious as always, but he was always willing to joke at any moment. We had a lot to catch up on, but our letters kept us up to speed on the main things in our lives.

That night, after the first session, we caught up. "So, what is ministry like there?" I asked.

"This fall, I've started taking speaking engagements at local churches. I've begun meeting once or twice a week with a language tutor to help ensure I'm communicating correctly and to continue learning the necessary phrases," he responded.

In his excitement, he told me about the European Youth Conference in the Spring of 1993.

"Are you doing WOL clubs in the churches too?" I asked.

"In September 1992, we held our first club in the village, attended by about 35 teens, mostly between the ages of 12 and 14, for a gym night. Afterward, we went to Dave James' house, where we had testimonies and refreshments. Since then, they have met up every Friday night."

He continued, "In the village, we have a leadership team of six, and two other clubs have started in nearby towns. Do you know what, Butler? We held our first Volleyball Marathon in November."

The castle grounds, the program, and the future BI were in the hands of other locals and missionaries. They supported one another in the areas where their ministries overlapped.

We quickly had breakfast together in the morning and then returned to our quiet times. The time was short but sweet; I lingered for another cup of tea. His dad, always up early, was there to chat. "We are thrilled to hear about your work in the Middle East; it is a real need." I looked at the Bubar fridge, saw my picture next to Dan's, and thanked him. His dad smiled and said, "Thanks so much for being a friend to Dan; he appreciates the good friend you have been to him."

After the day sessions in which we were both representatives of our respective mission boards, we could listen to each other's presentations. Dan was central to the conferences since the story of Hungary was the latest ministry miracle. In a break-out session, I shared the importance of making disciples in the Muslim world.

In the evening, we chatted again.

"Butler, what will you do for language?"

"Well, first, I need to learn survival local language and then study Farsi full-time."

He responded, "Language is a constant learning process. As Burt told us, 'An inch is a cinch, but a yard is hard.' This has proved to be true with the Hungarian language. Keep going is the hardest part.

"I hope you don't mind, but you and Stuart [our roommate at TTU] have both become sermon illustrations there in Hungary, so if you visit, you might want to go under an anonymous name. Although they might not recognize you anyway, with your beard." He joked.

"What are you saying?" I inquired.

"Oh, you know our typical fun stories of protests, selling Little Debbie cakes, and burning danishes."

"Embellished as usual?" I asked.

"Butler, would you expect anything else?"

Changing the topic, he asked, "So, have you found someone yet?"

"Well, you know what they say about seminary. It is like a cemetery for dating—every single woman there has at least ten guys pursuing them, while the other men have given up hope. I recall meeting one girl in a singles group. She said she wanted to go to the Middle East, and I shared with her that I had the same vision! But then, the next week in class, the teacher asked us all what our hopes for ministry were, And she said, 'I want to work with youth in the USA.' I'm fairly certain she was trying to distance herself from me. It was another, *Oh, that's nice, but I don't think so.*" That was a common phrase Dan and I repeated to each other whenever a woman in university gently said no to my request for a date.

"Butler, you know many others have gone before us single. Look at our former dormmate Mike Nicholes in Korea. The Lord will lead as we go in obedience. Our singleness is not a reason not to go."

"Bubar, do you remember at TTU when at the missions conference about 30 female students responded to the call to go to the mission field, but only six males? Then Dr. Jennings gave a focused invitation to the students, *Men, are you out there?*"

Bubar responded, "Yeah, he did this before the message because, the evening before, he saw that women responded but not men. I remember — he called them out for apathy and callousness. Just like Jack Wyrtzen said of Sophie Muller, she would not need to plant churches alone if men went to the Amazon jungle and served."[44]

He continued, "There are many nice girls at the Bible Institute, so just go and pick one."

"Yeah, right, Bubar. Just go there and choose one, right?" I was only a guest for a few days, and it did not seem possible. Yet his comments, which seemed foolish to me at the time, became prophetic.

Next Day

After breakfast with Dan, we went over to the BI. I recall sitting next to my display where literature on different world faiths lay on the table. A BI professor, Tom Davis, who had spent a year on sabbatical studying in Israel, picked up the booklet on Muslims. He had a year of contact with them there and wanted to see what we were saying. I felt that he always looked favorably on our type of work, as he had firsthand experience with many of the fundamental challenges of the Middle East. After the session, we discussed the relations between Muslims and Jews. My affinity with him began only then, as his sabbatical year had coincided with the year Bubar and I attended the Bible Institute.

Since I knew many in the overseas department and at the Bible Institute, I asked about doing a skit for our agency to promote our summer programs. I was there with Timothy Schultz, who worked with Hindus in the New York City area. We were part of the same agency and both graduates of Tennessee Temple University, so we connected well.

I suggested that most students are not yet considering long-term work, but they could consider summer training in NYC. During that decade, our mission had three training courses simultaneously. The focus was on learning about the teachings and methods to share with Muslims, Hindus, or East Asians (primarily Chinese). Typically, potential missionaries attend the training to prepare for one of these areas. So, the skit would focus on getting students to consider this.

I spoke with a small group of students about needing help with the skit. One of the dorm supervisors, Carmen, said, "Oh, you need to get Sharon Saunders; she is great at skits." So we found three students, including Sharon. In the skit, a guy mentioned how he met a Muslim while on open-air ministries in NYC and did not know how to talk to someone of that faith, so I suggested the summer training program. Another came up, which was Sharon, and she said that when she was on a singing tour with the Collegians, she met a Hindu, so Tim promoted the opportunity to work with them in NYC. Then, finally, Carmen came up and said she loved Chinese food, and I promoted the training with East Asians: a simple skit, but fun.

After the skit in the afternoon, Sharon came up to the display table and began chatting with me more. Previously, I'd noticed her as she was talking with Tim. As we spoke, and it was likely just small talk, her friend Frank, who was involved in the local church ministry with her, came up. Here is what Sharon had to say about this to me:

"Frank and I were in the same local church ministry on the weekends, and I was looking at the table. You were there, and you started chatting with me. Frank came along and looked back and forth at us like at a ping-pong game. It was very embarrassing. Then he reached between us, picked your prayer card off the table, and gave it to me.

"You know, a mere five months before I came to WOL, I would have said, 'No, thanks; I'm already praying for so many people I actually know.' I was very blunt, but I'd learned some manners at WOL, so I just said thank you, and took it. Back at my dorm, I stuffed it in my drawer. The other reason it didn't procure a place on my bulletin board was because I had just come to terms with the likelihood of being single forever, and I didn't want to be distracted by the picture of a handsome man who clearly had other plans. I was there to join WOL and go to the former Soviet Union."

The whole prayer card incident took me aback, and I did not ask her to sign up for my newsletter, which would have given me her address.

Dan's Inadvertent Set-Up

Dan said on the last day of the conference, "You need to put your name in to be a chapel speaker. Let's go over to Jack Wyrtzen's office and talk to him."

"Bubar, that is not going to happen. Are you crazy?"

"Butler, I know a few things and a few people. Let's go." So, reluctantly, I hopped into his car and we proceeded up the road to HQ. On our way, I thought, *What? No way*. But Dan did not take no for an answer, and his assurance convinced me.

"Bubar, you know I've never met Jack personally! I was in his home as a student, but there were about 15 other people there!"

"Uncle Jack will be glad to meet you," Bubar assured me, adding that he also knew the secretary. Since Jack was speaking elsewhere, it would be the secretary we would meet.

We walked into the office, and Dan gave the spiel about our friendship, my dedication to WOL Inn for many summers, and my call to ministry to the least-reached in the Middle East.

The secretary said, "Well, the schedule is set for the spring, but let me have your name just in case there is a cancelation." She took my name and number.

Also, we mentioned that I lived in Perth, only 80 miles away, so I could quickly come up and speak if needed. We left there, and I put it out of my mind. I thought, *They won't call me*.

Two weeks later, I got a call to speak for chapel at the beginning of February; they had an opening. *Wow, I thought Danny had influence*. I prayed and prepared to talk about Romans 15:20, my priorities for going to the least-reached.

Speaking at Chapel

Dan returned to Hungary, and it was time for me to speak in chapel. But the main event occurred the night before in Scotland dorm. Here is what Sharon had to say about that evening:

"It was study break, and I was at my desk when a bunch of our dormmates came in to talk to my personable roommate, Jana. The topic turned to good-looking guys on campus.

While Jana patiently listened, I recall being annoyed. Finally, I said, 'None of the guys on campus are good-looking; they're all vanilla.' My secret reason was that, whenever I read the Bible, I imagined Jesus with a beard, and it became my standard for attractiveness.

"But alas, beards were against WOL rules back then. I continued, 'This is my idea of good-looking.' Opening my drawer, I pulled out Jeff's prayer card from the back and showed it to the girls.

"At that point, Anne Sherman, another dormmate, said, 'Oh, him, I know that guy. He's in my local church ministry on weekends.' Something clicked, and I thought, *He's still in the area?* I said aloud, 'I thought he'd gone overseas already.' Anne said, 'No, he's at Perth Bible.'

"Well, the next day, they introduced the chapel speaker, and there, in the flesh, was the bearded man of prayer card fame! All my dormmates looked at me, cheering and giggling. I stared straight ahead, pretending not to be connected to the disruption."

Since the cheers of Sharon's dormmates blended into the welcoming applause, I did not realize what had just happened. I nervously began my message on Romans 15:20, discussing the sacrifices I made to go overseas and to reach the least-reached.

I mentioned prioritizing God over a relationship. Unknown to me, right before meeting me at the missions conference, Sharon had written to a guy friend back home, ending the relationship because he was not planning to go overseas for the long term. With that act of obedience, she felt she was also ending her last chance to have a relationship that might lead to marriage.

After chapel, I recall that Sharon was the main person who came up to offer some encouraging words. At that point, I was relieved to have finished my message before 500 students, and I greeted her, "Hey, Sharon Saunders!" She seemed surprised, but I knew her name because of Carmen's skit recommendation. Incidentally, her friend Carmen had recently given her a verse: *"No good thing does He withhold from those whose walk is blameless"* (Psalm 84:11), to help her understand that God's will, whether singleness or marriage, is a good thing. Sharon did not tell me then, but after I spoke at chapel, she started to pray for me.

Love in NYC while on WOL Outreach

That spring, I had many interactions with WOLBI, but conversations with Sharon, though pleasant, were rare and brief. I was still following Dan's advice to keep my eyes open for a potential spouse, and Sharon seemed to be hiding. Then, someone extended an invitation (possibly instigated by me) to join the school on its outreach in NYC. Dan encouraged me to go even though he had returned to Hungary. This was the first year the entire BI was going to Manhattan to witness, and it sounded like fun. Being sure they would meet Muslims there, I figured I might be of help, and I was allowed to join as a team member to reach Muslims.

When the time came, I stayed with Tim Schultz, who lived near NYC in New Jersey, while the BI students were at a hotel near Times Square. Every day, I traveled to Manhattan to serve with the teams, except for one day when I visited Hindus with Tim.

My days in NYC with the WOLBI outreach team turned out to be less adventurous than my day with Tim, in which he shared the gospel with a Brahman priest who was seeking. On the final day, however, our team did have a small adventure. Although I didn't know it at the time, God had planned an event that would change my life.

Elevator Appointments

Every morning, the groups would meet in the hotel lobby, and then go out onto the streets of NYC to share the gospel. On the last day of outreach, I arrived a bit early and spent the time chatting with a few acquaintances. Near the elevators, a man was speaking into the intercom to a group of people who appeared to be stuck in the elevator. He was telling them to be calm as help was on the way.

I thought nothing further of it, and went to meet my group, not far from there, on the upper level of the lobby. Everyone was there except one person. I mentioned the elevator incident and wondered if she was in it. Sure enough, after about 10 minutes, the missing student showed up and said she'd been stuck in the elevator. As we headed down, she began relaying the experience to her curious teammates.

Meanwhile, Sharon was on the lower level of the lobby, also waiting for a missing student. During the entire outreach, I had not seen her, but on the way down the escalator, there she was, wearing an orange shirt. I love the color orange. At the bottom, we greeted each other, and she was surprised to see me at her school's outreach. Our groups were still discussing the elevator, so Sharon and I started chatting. That summer, she was heading to WOL Europe for 3 weeks and would be visiting Hungary, and I was moving to the Middle East.

In those days, before Facebook, email, or any electronic means, good old snail mail or the telephone were the primary ways to stay in touch. I am not sure why we hadn't exchanged addresses before, but on this occasion, we decided to send each other our prayer letters, so we exchanged addresses. I figured it was a great way to get to know each other, and I even thought she could meet up with Dan. This marked the beginning of our writing relationship, which continued until we were married two years later.

Many years after our marriage and well into a decade, Sharon and I began discussing that day. I was unsure if I'd mentioned the elevator before, but the story came up on this occasion. I was amazed afresh by how God reached down and planned a way for us to exchange addresses. It was no mere chance encounter! In reality, this part of my life was one of many divine encounters that God had orchestrated, guiding me to live and love according to his will.

Youth Reachout 1993

Youth Reachout was established in 1989 and has expanded to many countries worldwide. One of the 1993 trips was to 3 countries in Eastern Europe — Romania, Hungary, and Poland — and would be led by Lou and Thelma Nicholes. Sharon was in that group. Their most extended stop was at Tóalmás Castle, Hungary, where Dan was. I had written both Sharon and Dan about each other and encouraged them to chat, which they did, briefly, about knowing me. And that was it!

The trip was not uneventful, though. The story that became folklore in our family began after the Youth Reachout group left Hungary. They were entering Poland in the middle of the night, but the four Canadians, one of whom was Sharon, were told they could not enter for some reason. This was a small and isolated border crossing.

The border guards said, "You all can go on, but not the Canadians." Someone woke Mr. Nicholes and informed him that the officers were getting the Canadians off the train. Immediately getting up, he told the Canadians to stay put, and then he approached the border guard. "It is either none of us or all of us. It is not four but seventy-four." By this time, others were beginning to wake up. "No, no," they said, "just the four Canadians need to get off; the rest of you can stay."

To show he was serious, Mr. Nicholes told the seventy-four to gather their luggage and start getting off the train. Removing four people would not have taken long or caused a big scene, but 74 with all their luggage was another story. The border guards were confused about why all these people were attempting to get off. They kept saying, "Only the Canadians need to get off, but the rest of you can stay!"

But Lou Nicholes was not about to strand four people alone at a border crossing. He bluntly and boldly repeated, "*Not four, but seventy-four,*" adding, "*and seventy-four pieces of luggage.*" The border officials realized he was serious and proceeded to try a different tactic. They took Lou back to their kitchen area and worked out the difficulty.

Eventually, Mr. Nicholes emerged, and the border officials announced, "Okay, the Canadians can go with the other seventy."

Recalling the incident, my wife said, "At the time, I was surprised that there was a game to play, that Lou Nicholes knew how to play the game, and that he played it."

Once the trip was over and I asked Dan about his meeting "my friend," he said, "*Without seeing a picture, I can't quite place Sharon Saunders. Was she here with Youth Reachout?*" (Oct. 14, 1994). With the large group size and the busyness of the activities, he missed their first encounter.

He had a passion for ministry and keeping busy. When he focused on things, he sometimes forgot his surroundings or, in this case, the person who would eventually become my wife. Once, he wrote, "This summer, I was at the airport, *and I left my address book on top of a telephone. When I came back for it several minutes later, then it was gone. I know that that's not a good excuse for not writing and keeping in contact, but it did play a part in it*" (Oct. 14, 1994). His focus could lead to forgetfulness and a lack of awareness in certain situations. Looking back, I am glad Dan did not fall for my wife. His obliviousness was my gain.

Chapter Twelve - Hungary Middle East Connection

"Say, where will you be moving to in [the Middle East]? Near the Iranian border?" (Oct. 28, 1992) Dan wrote. I went to the Middle East in August 1993. Like Dan, I went single and continued to pray about marriage. Focusing on language and ministry was our initial priority.

Thankfully, where I lived was connected by land to Hungary, so we planned to meet up. His initial letter to me stated, "Yes, come to Hungary anytime you want." So I planned from the beginning to make this happen.

Like Dan, I had someone I looked up to who influenced my decisions in ministry. Although I, too, learned a great deal from Harry Bollback, it was another visionary who pointed me in a new direction. I first received a letter from Pat Cate while in high school. He was a mobilizer for what would be known as Christar. I wrote asking about Muslim ministry, and he told me about the agency and invited me to their personnel training, not knowing I was still in high school.

Several years later, at DTS, I met with Dr. Cate on a few occasions and loved his vision for the work. He had since become president of Christar, and I sensed the agency was moving forward, especially with reaching the least-reached. For this mission, the least-reached were those without access to a church, so ministers needed to preach the gospel in the language of those desiring to reach—eventually, those who served established churches that worshipped in a manner relevant to the local culture.

As mentioned, my summer with the mission convinced me to join them. When I finally attended the New Personnel Orientation in 1992, I wanted to join a team heading to Central Asia, but that team was bound for one of the Turkish-based republics. My past was filled with Persians, and I felt a deeper connection to them as a people group. So, one evening, Pat, who encouraged us to use his first name, invited me out for ice cream.

On that ice cream outing, he suggested I work with Richard and Doreen Corley in the Middle East. I already knew them since they had come through TTU on at least one occasion, and Mr. Corley had also taught the summer training I attended in NYC. Pat further suggested that, while in the Middle East, I should survey a new work among Central Asian Persians. As we enjoyed our ice cream, he mentioned the benefit of being mentored by the Corleys and the freedom to explore a country where local churches were minimal or nonexistent. This plan, formulated over ice cream, became the path the Lord wanted me to follow.

In August 1993, I flew with the Corleys to the Middle East, and upon arrival, I realized life there was quite different. I recall the early Islamic call to prayer and praying to my heavenly father to work in the people's lives there.

Dan was in Hungary on the WOL landscape, and his father, Paul, was the Overseas Director during those days. Dan said, *"My mom is coming to help and do my room. Up until this time, it's been a bare-bones bachelor's pad, but they are painting it now and putting in a sink and shelves, etc. All that is missing is a Persian rug" (Oct. 3, 1993).*

He had found his niche: *"As I've already mentioned, the last two months have been incredibly busy. 5 camps at Tóalmás and one Klub Konference. As well as visiting churches, club leaders and friends to keep relationships good. Maybe it'll slow down for the summer…By the middle of March, we'll have 4 Bible clubs up and running. The Klub in Tóalmás is going well with a core group plus visitors" (Jan. 1994).*

Dan was so immersed in the language that it influenced his writing in English. Language was my first plan, too, but a trip to Hungary was also on the calendar.

My Trip to Hungary

The historical connection between the two locations was a part of my orientation. I read about the history of the Ottoman Empire and its ruler, Sulaiman the Magnificent, who conquered numerous countries in Eastern Europe. For this reason, Dan said, the Hungarians did not fondly regard that part of history they shared with some regional countries.

Bubar's focus on food led me to believe that he thought I was living in a desert, *"They have everything in Budapest. Pizza Hut, Wendys, Burger King, McDonald's, Kentucky Fried, Duncan Donuts, plus a wide variety of Hungarian restaurants, stores, appliances, you name it" (Oct. 3, 1993).* Whether or not Dan frequented these places would remain to be seen. My location had these eateries too, except for Wendys and donuts of any kind. I thought maybe we would party and eat out a lot. Yet we both were poor and did not have much money. I did not bring him a Persian rug; I had no money. Concerning these great places to eat, we went out only once.

I decided on February because Dan said, *"March is a Big Club month. April is a month for preparing for camp — with training sessions and conferences. May is full of camps" (Jan. 1994).* With this list, I knew he would be busy.

He was thrilled with all that was happening and knew he was in the right place, *"Grade schools have registered for Forest camps at Tóalmás. Depending on the school principal, we can even share the gospel in an evangelistic-style meeting. So now we are camping more and more" (Jan. 1994).*

He also listed some planned events, including the Euro-Youth event in Germany from March 31 to April 4.[45] In his letter, he invited me to join him. Still, he warned that the event was filling up quickly, with over 100 youths already registered. Connecting the ministry in Hungary with other nearby countries continued as a central part of the ministry there. Later, due to its use of English in the program, the Bible Institute in Hungary enabled students from throughout Europe to attend, thereby influencing the entire region.[46]

Dan ended his letter with, *"Check out the plane and train tickets…. Come to Hungary, Jeff!"* I was deeply immersed in Persian language study, but every three months, I had to leave the country I lived in to update my tourist visa, so I decided to head to Hungary for my second trip abroad.

I wish I had taken his advice and bought a plane ticket. Instead, I decided I wanted to see the Eastern European landscape. One Friday afternoon in February, I hopped on the bus, hoping to arrive in Budapest the following day. After only an hour on the road, we hit an ice storm. We passed another bus that had flipped onto its side and lay totaled while its passengers stood along the side of the road, trying to keep warm. *I prayed, Lord, keep us safe!* We had a long way to go — 25 hours — but I looked forward to arriving in Budapest Saturday afternoon in time for a nice supper with Dan.

The weather had caused me some concern, but it soon cleared up. Nevertheless, the bus continued to stop for almost any reason the driver deemed expedient.

In Bulgaria, the bus driver needed to stop to buy cheese. The country is known for its cheese, and the opportunity to purchase cheap, good, homemade cheese was apparently too good to pass up. I wasn't too impressed and thought others would feel the same, but everyone got up to buy cheese! The only ones left on the bus were an Australian couple and myself. We were dumbfounded that Bulgarian cheese was the Black Friday special. We reasoned that maybe this was the rest stop for supper, but it wasn't, since we stopped for tea and food one hour later.

During the tea break, they began unloading much of the bus's cargo — approximately 50 small boxes. As time stretched on, I began to wonder if this was really the main road to Budapest. I know that I specifically asked for the express bus and that they sold me the ticket, assuring me that it was.

I could not sleep. It was about two o'clock in the morning, and I was pretty ticked and overwhelmed. I got off the bus to see what they were dropping off. Much to my surprise, it was alcohol. *Wow, I was on a bootlegging bus.* Back on the bus, we could see the bus company staff inside the tea shop, playing music and dancing. We obediently sat on the bus, waiting for the party to come to an end.

For those living overseas, the trials of our faith are often simply cultural normalcies that, to the foreigner, seem unjust, where we find ourselves at the mercy of others. My blood was boiling, and my Christian faith was tested. Tired of waiting, I got out again and sarcastically asked, *Is this really the express bus? Let's go, Let's go!*

Finally, we left, and by early Saturday morning, we found ourselves at the border where the Danube River separates Romania and Bulgaria. Perhaps if I had known it was the famous Danube, I could have appreciated the glamour of my situation, but I didn't. The river flows to Budapest, so at least I was headed in the right direction, but I did not know that either.

We would need a ferry. Testing our patience once again, the ferry finally arrived, and the vehicles drove onto the shore. To my disappointment, however, it left without taking any cars or buses. After another long wait, a second ferry came and unloaded its vehicles. We were at the beginning of the line, so our chances of success were high. We waited expectantly to board and then watched helplessly as the second ferry pulled away from the shore, empty. *Argh!* I thought, *Bubar, you have no idea what trouble I'm going through to see you.*

A half-hour later, a third ferry docked and unloaded. As we inched expectantly toward the barge, the ferry staff jumped out and stopped all the vehicles. At this point, I was thoroughly upset.

How frequently do we expect circumstances to go our way? How often do we try to "drive" our situation instead of recognizing that we are not the Driver but "along for the ride"? You may be expecting a story of prayer, trusting the Lord, sharing the gospel with a fellow passenger, or a touching, cultural revelation. It is a pity that none of these great ideas occurred to me. I was disappointed and frustrated, like everyone else.

So, the forbidden barge sat there empty, and half an hour later, another one showed up and emptied. It seemed that Romania was quite successful in transporting, while Bulgaria was becoming the clear winner in vehicle count. Our bus moved forward, eventually paid the fare, and we got on. Once on the other side, they checked our documents, and we were finally on our way. It had taken over six hours to cross the Danube, which, by the way, appeared neither beautiful nor blue on that cold day, as the classical song is titled.

We passed about 8-10 miles of semi-trucks, lined up back-to-back to cross the border. I realized many people had waited much longer than I had to cross the Danube River border. And, as an express bus, we were prioritized.

How like life. We do not see the plan ahead, and so we worry. But God knows the plan, and we can always trust Him to see us through it, no matter how different it may look from our expectations.

I would not get to Budapest on time. After another snowstorm, potentially criminal passengers, policemen, more stops, and a bribe, I crossed into Hungary around midnight, Saturday night.

I was supposed to meet up with Dan between 5 and 7 p.m. In those days, we had no cell phones, and I hadn't seen any pay phones along the way, so I couldn't contact him.

Dan and a Hungarian friend went to Budapest to pick me up. At the bus station, Dan asked about buses coming from the East. They said those buses don't stop there. He and his friend walked around the station but could not find me. He was quite worried and wondered where the bus would drop off its passengers. He visited a few more key locations where passing buses might drop off passengers, but I hadn't arrived yet. He stayed until about 11 p.m. looking for me but eventually returned to the castle for the night. He prayed and committed the situation to the Lord.

I had hoped to hear Dan preach the next day, but Sunday came, and I was still on my journey. Meanwhile, Dan spoke at a local church and then returned to the castle to assess the situation. When the bus finally arrived in Budapest, it did not head to the bus station but instead drove around the city's suburbs to find a suitable drop-off location. When I say "suitable," I mean a convenient location for the bus staff, not for us getting off. Eventually, they let the Australian couple and me off at a bus stop on the outskirts of the city.

Adventure in Budapest

I was thankful to be in Budapest, but I had no idea where I was, nor did I know any Hungarian. But God showed his mercy in many ways. For one, there had been a place to exchange money at the border between Romania and Hungary, so I at least had cash. Also, I was not alone. The best part was that we were dropped at a tram stop. Budapest was known for its extensive tram system, and this line went to the central bus station. So, we made it to the station, where we parted ways, and I went inside to find directions to Word of Life Hungary.

I knew Dan would not be looking for me at that time because he'd said he would be preaching at church. It was 9 a.m. and I had a choice. I could sit in the station for six hours until he arrived, since he would most likely return to Tóalmás before heading into the city. Or, as I decided, I could go to him. I had sat on the bus for 40 hours; I was not about to sit for six more. But what was the address?

As a die-hard Word of Lifer, I traveled with a Word of Life Quiet Time. In those days, the addresses of their international locations were listed inside. I was pleased to find the Tóalmás location, and I showed it at the information booth. They directed me with a few written notes to take the metro, a train, and then a bus to the village. I recruited locals to guide me through every step, showing me the way.

At the train station, I had two hours to wait before my train left and, recalling Dan's praise of all the good food in Hungary, I bought some pizza from a kiosk just outside the station. Sadly, the sauce was ketchup, and it was cold. So when I discovered a McDonalds nearby, it was like finding the Waldorf Astoria. I settled in with my Quiet Time journal, enjoying the warmth after my stressful trip. I thanked God for getting me to Budapest and convicting me of my bad attitude.

Finding Bubar

I boarded the train to Tóalmás, happy to be on my way. There were 20 stops to get where I needed to go, but once on the train, I did not see Tóalmás on the list. So I started to write down the names of the stations and asked someone which one went to Tóalmás. One kind Hungarian lady said to go to Tapioszecsoe — yes, that is the name. I could not even attempt to pronounce it, so when the kind lady got off, I was left wondering how I would tell anyone I needed to get to Tapioszecsoe. My respect for Dan's language ability was growing.

I didn't know where the train had just stopped, and I became pretty anxious. Then, I discovered that the names of the stops were written above each platform. I moved to a better spot to see and found my stop was still five stations away.

Arriving at the stop about 45 minutes after I had started, I walked up to some people at a bus stop across the road. When I showed the WOL address, someone suggested getting on the 486, but the 487 appeared instead. Another friendly Hungarian mentioned that 487 would work. On the bus, I asked the driver about the address, and he assured me he would tell me when to get off. (It was the second village on the bus route. I sat near him, and after about 20 minutes, he said, "This is Tóalmás."

As I was getting close, I remembered that I had prayed at the train station for God to keep Dan at the castle so we wouldn't be in two separate places. *Lord, keep him at the castle; may he not return to Budapest.*

On the bus, one man who knew little English recruited a teenager who was getting off at the same station. He motioned for me to follow him. I figured this teenager would point me in the general direction and be on his way. However, surprisingly, he walked me right up to the gate of the WOL camp. Throughout the journey, the Hungarian people consistently demonstrated kindness and helpfulness.

A long entrance road led to the castle where I knew Dan lived, so I went directly to it. He had sent me pictures, and it was impressive, but there was no one around. So I walked in. Still, no one was around. I walked up a set of stairs and was about to yell out, "Bubar, where are you?" However, I heard someone in the corridor, and when I turned the corner, I was face to face with Dan. He was the first person I saw on the property.

He said, "Butler, where have you been? I've been so concerned for you. We visited the main bus terminal last night, and they informed us that no buses from your location stop there. I was so worried."

"Praise the Lord, I finally made it! I'm so glad to be here."

"You know, they say these buses from outside the country just drop people off in the middle of nowhere. I even called the Embassy to see if you were found. Buses from the Middle East are illegal here."

Dan had just returned from church and was talking to his friend about finding me. He said he was about to leave in 10 minutes, but I arrived just in time. It was a crazy journey, but the Lord was in it all. It's kind of like life.

We enjoyed almost a week together and reminisced about our common memories. We shared the joys and challenges of ministry and prayed for one another. My time in Budapest was awesome. Pleasant memories are sometimes like 20/20 vision in that nothing mars the recollections. But my trip was traumatic. Like most people who work overseas, I could now fill an entire book with travel mishaps, but this was among my first, and it made a lasting impression. Essentially, I am saying that I remember it in more detail than I do my time spent with Dan.

Even though the trip had cost me a day, visiting the site and staying in the castle for even a few days was a privilege and an honor. To see firsthand God's miracle of opening a door to ministry in that land, at a former communist campground, showed the power of God's hand in the process.

1993 picture showing where Dan's room was at the WOL Castle

Another Talk

"How do you like it here?" I asked.

Dan said, "I love it. I was made for this. Are you sure you don't want to join us?"

"The Persian church in my country amazes me. Seeing 40 Persians celebrate Christmas — about half of them for the first time — there's nothing better than that."

"God works in these oppressed areas and does the unexpected," he said.

"For the celebration, my language tutor pressured me into doing a skit with him. I was one of the wise men and had to say in Persian, *'Look, there is a shining star.'* Many of these Iranians believe the wise men were from their country, so now, like them, they celebrate the birth of Christ for the first time."

Bubar replied, "Yeah, ministry here is more than a job. It's a resolve. I know Christ has invited me here, and I want to share him with the Hungarians. It is my destined place to accomplish his will."

"When I think about God's plan, it's like we are pieces on a chessboard. He knows what the next move is, but often we don't," Bubar said.

"Ain't that the truth," I responded.

Years later I was reminded of how differently others saw overseas work. Upon arriving, I worked alongside other foreigners to provide humanitarian relief. I recall one person stating that he came there to gain international work experience for his resume. He believed that a stint overseas would give him an edge in securing a job. For Dan and me, we were not there for resume purposes or social status but because God had planted a focused drive in our hearts.

But another missionary said, "Yeah, but if your resume says you stayed there over five years, in the West they would say, 'What happened? Did you go native?' At that point, longevity gives a negative impression."

Not wanting to become so out of touch, I wrote to Greg Parsons, who has served many years in mission strategies. He summed up our Christian calling, saying, "I believe we are all called to God's global purposes. No matter our role — frontlines or local — NOR the way ("supported" global workers or business or a job)... No matter WHAT or HOW we do it, we should all be focusing our lives/prayers/efforts to seeing the Kingdom come in people's lives" [emphasis original]. Dan and I recognized God's global purposes and desired to see how He would use us.

Ministry at the Castle

Others who visited the castle left with similar impressions. The international director of Word of Life, Don Lough, Jr., said, "I remember visiting Dan in Hungary, and he seemed so happy and fulfilled. But above all, I remember Dan as a young man who desired to have his life count for Jesus Christ."

Robin Brooks said, "I remember visiting the Word of Life Hungary camp with my parents in its early years. He [Dan] was already fluent in the language and ran camp just like WOL Island, crazy fun and yet serious. I don't know what message he preached the night of the campfire, but nearly the whole camp went forward for some kind of decision. Very moving."

His pastor and wife, Roger and Judy Ellison, said after visiting the ministry at the castle, "We were thrilled and elated by the time there, especially because the electricity of Daniel Bubar cut our hearts."[47]

Being in Hungary reminded me of what gives Word of Life its unique character. It is not just a place or program, but people. I recall that during the summer of 1986, I arrived at the Inn early to work for a few weeks, preparing it for the season. They had some weekend guests, but the desolation of the place gave me the sense that it was the people who made the place what it was. Although I was at one of my favorite places, I still felt lonely. Now, being with Dan again brought joy, comradery, and friendship.

His encouragement and advice prompted me to finish well and take the next challenge by its horns, which was studying language. Yet in order to do that, I needed to get back to my location.

Yugoslavia Train

When it was time to return, I did not want another wild bus adventure. Some recommended the train since it went straight to my country without going through Romania, but it went through Yugoslavia.

I remember the dreadful feeling about this passage. It was February 1994, and the Bosnian war was still going on in Yugoslavia. Though UN peacekeeping forces attempted to avoid war, no peace treaty had been negotiated. The train line traveled from Hungary through Belgrade, today's Serbia, and then to Sofia, Bulgaria. I was unfamiliar with geography, and internet access was not available back then. So, I took the train, knowing by faith that it would be a good way to travel back.

To buy the ticket, I needed a Yugoslavian visa to avoid denial at the border, so Dan helped me obtain this permission at the embassy.

On the train, I found a nice compartment, and I was the only one in the room. The first part was overnight, so I arrived in Yugoslavia in the morning. I was enjoying my privacy and not being bothered by others. While sitting there, a conductor asked me to reserve my seat for about three dollars. I thought that was strange. No one was on this train, and I needed to reserve my seat.

When we entered the first central station in Yugoslavia, I looked out the window, and a massive crowd of people were running toward our train. On this trip, I learned that a train ticket costs only one dollar from one end of the country to the other, while a bus ticket for the same eight-hour trip was about $20. So, everybody took the train. Well, I had paid much more than that for my ticket and, on top of that, had to reserve my seat for three more dollars.

The train was packed by then, and fearing I would lose my luggage and my seat, I sat for hours without moving. Yet my bladder could no longer hold on. I pondered my baggage and realized that even if I lost my clothes and small items to a thief, it would be worth it if I could find a bathroom. When nature calls, true priorities take precedence. Snaking through the crowded corridor, I finally found the small restrooms, only to discover that they were locked. In each was a passenger who decided that was the best-isolated place to sit for this eight-hour trip through the country. I returned to my seat and surveyed my belongings to ensure I had not lost anything.

When we neared Bulgaria's border, the train emptied again. Then, at what I assume was the border of Bulgaria, the conductor returned. Now, he wanted me out of this seated area. I couldn't understand why since I had paid for the seat. If he wanted me to move, then I expected to get my money back. My American idea of justice told me I needed to fight for some personal freedom and claim some rights. How often over the years has my Americanness taken over, and I expect specific outcomes that will benefit me.

Christ made himself of no reputation, and he denied privileges he was worthy of—a lesson I have continually learned over the years. The conductor seemed to want his friend in the room and tried to kick me out. I wish I had been less culture-shocked and more of a witness on/during my travels.

A discussion took place, but the conductor did not understand English. As I insisted on a refund, I misunderstood the situation. While my ticket stated it was valid for 24 hours, he informed me it was only good for 500 kilometers, which we had surpassed. Realizing I wouldn't win the argument, I decided to move on.

Why do we argue? I've noticed that my defense of personal privileges often becomes the focus of discussions. I worry that others perceive me as unattractive and feel entitled to something when I experience "rip-off rage," believing someone is trying to take advantage of me. This insecurity heightens my emotions. Feeling inadequate for the situation pumps the adrenaline. I wish I could adopt a mindset more aligned with Christ—something I clearly failed to do in this situation.

I moved up a few rooms, joining a German couple and a woman from South Africa. I had been alone for long enough and was eager to engage in some non-confrontational communication. The ride, at least, was straightforward and continued consistently toward our destination.

But one of our friends returned and reported that no other train cars were behind us; a dozen or so cars had detached. (This is the reason I had to move.) Once again, my misunderstanding veiled an altruistic purpose. We felt like we were in a Hitchcock movie where the lady vanished, but now the train was down to three parts: the engine, a first-class warm section, and then our car.

One passenger went forward but was stopped. The car ahead was full of a tour group from Russia, and they had the heat on. We, on the other hand, were in a walk-in freezer.

It was February, and the weather was quite chilly. We requested that the heat be turned on, and the conductor agreed, but nothing changed. We then realized the train had stopped in a remote area surrounded by fields.

This stop, located in the middle of the fields, took about 1.5 to 2 hours. The train sat there, and nothing happened, leaving us unsure of its meaning. We eventually arrived 3-4 hours later than scheduled, but this was much better than the 14 hours the bus took, and I was glad to finally be home.

Hog Wild Language Lab

By the fall of 1993, I began my daily grind of disciplined language study. Dan encouraged me, *"Hope all is going well with you and your studying of the language. It really is import[ant] to get"* (Oct. 3, 1993).

At that time, I was a pre-K in language, and Bubar was quite fluent in Hungarian. Indeed, there were times I felt like quitting. Then I could hear Bubar's words, "The two reasons for quitting are if God moves you into something else or if you die." Well, language was a do-or-die situation for us. Do it and learn the language so that ministry can happen. This was God's call on our lives, and conquering this mountain was necessary.

Individual helpers came to my house a few days a week. One helper said he had to go to work at 9 a.m., so I offered him the chance to teach me early. At 6:30 a.m., he appeared at my door for a two-hour class. Then he left for work. However, soon enough, he started to come later and later, and on some days, he would fall asleep while teaching me or while I was reading something. My class bored him and put him to sleep.

Dan began learning Hungarian in the fall of 1989. *"I'm also learning some Hungarian. It's like studying for quiz team"* (Jan. 30, 1990). A few years later, he was teaching and preaching in it. In Dan's September 1991 letter, he shared his language adventures with me: *"My social life? Well, I'm on the verge of being able to hold a meaningful conversation in the language, and I guess this means I can do more than just keep my eyes open. There are nice gals here, but I also realized that I'm not dating here like in high school or the B.I. or even Temple [TTU], for that matter.*

"The next gal I 'date' I'd like to 'date for keeps.' This makes me take a good hard look and want to get the language better to really know someone. I believe by Christmas I'll be close to fluent, whatever that is. Next summer I want to preach in Hungarian."

God called him and made him Hungarian. He was motivated in this area because he knew that knowing the language would make him the most effective in ministry. His ministry was unto God, so he wanted to give it his all. And perhaps he wanted to get to know a Hungarian woman.

With these multiple motivations, he strove for fluency through intense effort and time prioritization. He pressed on no matter how hard it was. Anyone who has attempted to learn a new language knows the patience and humility needed for the task. Dan had to humble himself in his efforts to learn Hungarian.

He continued, *"Last night I translated for Eric at the testimony meeting and the only real mistake I made was saying pray 'to Eric' instead of 'for Eric,' however, my 8-12 yr. old audience was quick to correct me. As only they can do"* (Sept. 1991).

His eight-year-old crowd were not shy about correcting him. It can be embarrassing to be corrected by a child, yet Dan responded with laughter and thankfulness. In moments of discouragement, Dan would remind himself of the rewards that come with learning a new language. He knew he could look at the past and see how much easier certain aspects of the language had become. When he saw that he was growing, he was encouraged to keep pushing forward. God was working in him to prepare him for the ministry at hand.

Eventually, Dan's devotion to learning Hungarian started to affect his English. He wrote: *"They had an exhibit right next to ours. He did a demonstration of open-air preaching, writing Hungarian words on the paintboard, and he spelled the first word (love) wrong, but it is a common mistake that Amerikans make with this one letter. Everyone got a big chukkle out of it, and Matt handled it real well."* As Hungarian is a phonetic language, Dan began implementing its spelling in his English writing, especially with the letter "K," and no longer worried about misspelling English words.

Later, when I began studying language, I asked Dan, "What should I do about language? How should I approach it?"

Dan said, "Butler, go hog wild for as long as possible. When you feel you can no longer persevere, persist and keep studying.

"Go Hog Wild! — Take in the language and hang out with those who speak it. Even after work, I hang out with the castle workmen and listen to them speaking Hungarian. I attempt to speak and let them correct me."

He listened to their colloquial conversations and attempted to master speaking this difficult language. He developed a daily habit of spending a lot of time and listening to the language.

His words rang in my ears, especially since I was studying Persian, the primary language of Shia Muslims. Although I couldn't use the phrase "hog wild" with much success, I adopted Dan's attitude toward language study.

"What else?" I asked.

"Laugh at yourself, and don't take yourself too seriously. A person who can learn like a child and laugh at mistakes has the advantage," he counseled.

I, too, had my share of silly mess-ups during learning and teaching times. Soon after my first term, one of my first messages was to a small group of Iranians in Dallas. I wanted to emphasize how Jesus said he was the first and the last in the Revelation 1 passage. I looked out, and one of the ladies I taught the Bible to in English during my seminary years looked on with a smile. I thought she must be proud that I could now speak her language.

Afterward, I asked her thoughts about what I said, thinking she was a safe person to ask. She said, "I was smiling because it was quite humorous that you said Jesus is the Grass and the Last! I didn't know he was the grass!"

Oh, I thought, how embarrassing. What a joke. I needed to be in the audience and not upfront. My audience was more polite than Dan's. These two words were so close, and my vowel shift in the words made me say "Jesus was the Grass and the Last."

"Anything else?" I asked Dan.

"Spend time with the people and learn how they express themselves. Try to interact with them, but listen more," Bubar said.

Michael Frost, a missiologist, once said, "If you have limited relational ability, then your missional effectiveness will be limited." Dan's proximity to those around him provided him with an open door to learn from them, hear their concerns, and minister to them.

It was a lesson not to be forgotten, and I learned to laugh at my mistakes and apply Bubar's language methods. Yet his intensity intimidated me, and Mike Loftis with ABWE said about Dan that he "astounded all of us with his phenomenal ability to smoothly and eloquently speak the Hungarian language. Gifted by God to fill a special role with Word of Life."

I went wild, with two-hour classes five times a week, studying about 40-50 hours a week. I planned visits to the homes of refugees or invited one or another in after my private lessons. Also, I attended church meetings in the language at least twice a week. Gradually, I learned the language well enough to begin ministry.

I looked forward to the future, like Dan, who wrote: *"Study is intensive as I'm sure it is for you too… Learning another language is brutal, but almost just as rewarding, no more so, cause you [will] forget how hard it was in the future"* (Oct. 1991). He then credited the Lord for his help. *"My 'services' have become of much greater*

value since the language came much easier for me. I even
surprised myself. Of course, the Lord has been looking out for the
little baker boy from the Bubar & Butler Baker summer of 1980
[1982]. Wow! Does that ever sound ancient" (Oct. 28, 1992).

Enduring in Language

I had numerous private language helpers, and after my sleepy helper was dismissed, I invited another to help me. He became a great helper, but he loved garlic and always gave me the traditional three-kiss greeting. The smell was overpowering, but I did not want to offend him. After a few weeks, though, I suggested we put off the morning kisses as we see each other every day. He appeared slightly offended, and I most likely made a cultural mistake, but my relief superseded any regret.

Over the years, some of the best advice I received, besides Dan's, was from David Hunter, who taught a group of us in the Central Asia Study Center. He stressed focusing on one subject at a time and learning to contrast ideas to expand one's vocabulary.

He said that when one is in the intermediate stage of language acquisition, one learns to define words using other words in the language, rather than relying on an English dictionary. So, I found a Farsi-to-Farsi dictionary to use as my first resource. Also, I made language cards with definitions written in Farsi.

When I began teaching a text, I followed his advice and focused on studying it in the local language first. Many people make the mistake of starting with their mother tongue and continue to rely on it, which leads to a process of translation rather than a proper understanding of the target language.

My wife, gifted in language learning, can hear the intonation of a language, along with how a word is stressed. Most likely, her musical ability aided her language studies. However, auditory subtleties tend to elude me, and as a result, my ability to imitate the language is limited. Yet God helps each of us in this learning process.

Granted, today, there are numerous helpful apps and techniques for learning a language, but the bottom line is that it still depends on hard work and perseverance.

Chapter Thirteen - Last Time with Dan

After a year of writing, Sharon and I were both going to be in upstate New York at the same time. In 1994, my wife was an appointee with WOL, and Paul Bubar was the overseas director. This combination brought some trepidation in my heart.

Avoiding the Bubars

During our brief visit together in June 1994, we were able to spend three days together. But before returning to the Middle East, I called Don Lough, Jr., who was working under Paul Bubar, to let him know I was interested in one of their appointees. I asked him to keep this information to himself until something came of it.

If something did, we had no intention of keeping it from the Bubars, but Sharon was at WOL all summer, and I did not want to expose her to any teasing, especially since we were still figuring out how serious we were.

I cannot say for sure if Mr. Bubar would have teased her, but I knew him to be a jokester. I reasoned I would tell them when the relationship grew more serious.

In September 1994, only weeks before our engagement, Sharon met with Wayne Lewis, who served in the overseas office, particularly with appointees. He and Sharon discussed sending out another letter to supporters to move the process forward and facilitate travel to Argentina. In the end, Sharon said, by the way, she was heading to London and would meet up with a guy she was writing to…. At this point, Mr. Lewis placed his pen down and looked up. He wisely said, "Let's wait until you come back before we send this letter out."

"Oh, don't worry about that," she said. "Our furloughs won't match up for another eight years." Mr. Lewis smiled and said, "Nevertheless, I think we should wait."

Sharon was heading to London to see her sister, and I was heading there for a networking conference about Central Asia. We spent about twelve days together. When I left the Middle East, I had no intention of getting engaged, but love persuaded me.

Besides my attraction to her, we shared a similar context: our WOL connection and calling toward full-time ministry drew us closer.

We brought out the best in each other and desired to serve and please the Lord. We were spiritual companions on a similar journey and wanted to spend our lives together.

But alas, the engagement had moved forward, and the Bubars did not even know I was dating! I was back in the Middle East, but in NY, Sharon told her friends. Soon afterward, one of them happened to be with a WOL ladies' group and mentioned our engagement. Though many were surprised, none expressed it as thoroughly as Shirley Bubar. She walked around saying our names over and over, wondering, "How in the world did I not know about this?" Now, she was always thrilled to hear about a new engagement, but because she had been like a mother to me during our college years, keeping my intentions from her was almost a betrayal.

Yet, in this situation, which happened quite quickly for us, I could not see another option.

Are you prepared?

Our engagement demonstrated some of my intensity and difficulty expressing myself. Communicating clearly has always been a challenge. Before, we only communicated through written words, giving me time to consider my questions or responses carefully. Now, together in person, I was having a hard time finding words that matched my intentions.

I wanted to emulate a speaker Dan and I had heard at the Bible conference back in 1983. Georgi Vins, a Baptist pastor who endured years of suffering in a Russian prison during the Soviet Union era, shared how he asked his wife to marry him: "Are you prepared to go with me to prison and, if necessary, to death? If so, will you marry me?" I didn't anticipate facing such serious consequences, but at that moment, I was fully committed to serving the Lord in the former Soviet Union. Dan and I sat together at this conference, and when we heard his testimony, it left a deep impression on us. That weekend, I also dedicated my life to missions.

So, when considering engagement, I thought of his testimony. On the streets of London, I planned my big moment. I asked Sharon, "Are you prepared to go to Central Asia?" She thought briefly and then said, "No, I'm not, but if God were to call me, I would go." I was trying to propose and she said No. This was not good. I tried to rephrase my question, "No, I mean with me? Are you prepared to go with me?" Still unclear if this was a proposal or not, she simply gave me an affirming hug, without actually saying yes. I, too, became unclear if we were engaged or not. So I stated plainly, "I want to marry you! I love you." It was supposed to be a question, but she understood and finally said the word "Yes." Communication has continued to be an adventure ever since.

The Georgi Vins method did not work the way I intended. Yet I still managed to get engaged, and we were planning on going to Central Asia. After the engagement, I wrote to Dan and told him that Sharon and I were engaged. He wrote, "Congratulations!!!!!! WOW!!!!! Good news travels fast. Don and Darla [Lough, Jr.] were just here, and they told me that you were getting serious with someone, but I didn't know that it was that serious. I guess it was your eyes, you know what my grandmother used to say….Well, as I read your letter you write that Sharon met your folks and that you went to England and met her mom and sis. You asked her to marry you without meeting her dad?[48] You also wrote that you decided to ask her to marry you before you left, and that you are engaged to be married May 20, 1995. I take it she said, 'Yes.' Butler, you left out a lot in your letter. How did you propose? How long have you known her for? When did you guys first meet? Etc." *(Oct 14, 1994).* His words conveyed how he rejoiced in my good fortune and also my continued challenge to communicate more thoroughly.

In my excitement, I didn't write out the details, but for Sharon and me, just being on the same continent and in the same country became quite challenging. Our few days together were filled with conversation and enjoying each other's company. By the time of our engagement, we had been writing for about a year and a half but had spent only 12 days together in person. Until I returned for our wedding preparations, we continued to write, and we upped our regular phone calls to once a week.

Concerning my engagement, Dan joked, "Well, Butler, it appears that you have outrun me in the race to the altar. I write "appears" because one never knows. I'm happy for you and know that this is God's answer for a real need in your life." At this point, he hinted he was interested in someone in Hungary but was still unsure how to proceed.

Answer to my Daily Prayer

My daily prayer for a wife, if God had one for me, reminded me that my dependence and expectation were in the Lord. A key verse was Psalm 62:5—"My expectation is from the Lord." I prayed and waited for him to lead me to her.

In the summer of 1982, I began to pray daily for my future wife, if the Lord had one for me. I prayed for her for six years before she even **knew** the Lord. Although she was not a Christian when I started, I believe my prayers played a part in drawing her to know the Lord. I did not meet her until about five years after her conversion. Praise the Lord that he hears our prayers. It was also miraculous that she ended up in my old stomping grounds: WOLBI.

My wife is from midwestern Canada. In the spring of 1992, WOLer Bob Parschauer visited his home province of Saskatchewan to preach in local churches, promoting WOL's ministry in the Eastern Soviet Bloc countries. He mentioned the need for teachers there. As a new believer and a teacher, my future wife-to-be thought this would be an excellent opportunity to pursue.

To provide perspective on this connection, Bob Parschauer, along with Chuck Kosman, visited churches in Hungary prior to the establishment of WOL Hungary. When Paul Bubar visited Hungary in 1982, Bob joined him from Germany and was used by God to help establish a presence in the country. Bob ministered for many years in Germany but also visited many Eastern European countries, including Hungary. He was from Saskatchewan, and so was Sharon.

He did not know it then, but when this young teacher came to ask about serving in Eastern Europe, his positive response encouraged her to apply to join WOL.

When Sharon came to Christ in 1988, she was studying French in Quebec to teach French immersion in Saskatchewan. In her initial class was a fellow prairie girl, Marlene, who befriended her. Sharon usually avoided Christians, but Marlene seemed "cool." A few days later, Sharon was moved to a class filled with a group of missionaries from the Christian Missionary Alliance (CMA). They were part of an experimental semester where future missionaries would polish their French in Quebec before moving to French-speaking Africa. As far as we know, that was the only year CMA sent them there. Marlene continued to witness to Sharon and gave her a Bible. Seven years later, she would be Sharon's maid of honor.

When Sharon put her faith in Jesus, her classmates were role models, and she believed all Christians should be missionaries.

Teachers in the former Soviet Union, yeah, this could be God's will. She approached Mr. Parschauer after he spoke at her church in Swift Current and expressed her interest in teaching in the former

Soviet Union. Pamphlet in hand, she contacted WOL and eventually enrolled in their MIT (Missionary in Training) program to prepare for overseas service. Eventually, they appointed her to go to Argentina because she was single and new in her faith.

At MIT, they suggested she needed Bible training, so she asked if they had a Bible School. Miraculously, a Saskatchewan believer who lived in the middle of the Bible Belt of Western Canada came to non-Christian upstate New York to study the Bible. She was oblivious about all the Bible Institutes in her province. Yet, again, it seemed that these prayers had a solid draw to get her to New York. All her friends thought she was crazy to go to New York to study the Bible. This made sense retrospectively, but God had a more excellent plan for her. God orchestrated her path and brought us together so we could meet. How awesome is that! It is better than any of my plans, and God did it!

When we were engaged, my future sister-in-law said to Sharon, "Why are you going to Central Asia? I have a friend whose husband is a photographer, and he often goes on long trips, but she stays home where she has a life. If it's husband's thing, let him do that and you stay home." What she didn't understand was that mission work is not a job or an overseas occupation. One leaves one's country and settles in a different community to make a spiritual difference. We both felt an urge to go, and granted, we knew it could be a short-term or long-term thing. For us this was the path which our marriage moved us forward on.

My Non-Word of Life Call

Do not think I ignored Word of Life; I often thought about serving with them. Before the summer of 1986, I met with WOL missionary Ernie Hautala, who was deeply interested in researching the WOL ministry into Indonesia, with Keith Ebrahim. I knew Keith because he had often taught me theology individually, during the summer of 1981, when we both worked at the Inn. Ernie asked me if I was interested in helping start Indonesia with Keith. We discussed church planting, which was not part of the WOL program at that time. That night, I wrote, "I am learning church planting but feel comfortable with WOL as an organization except about this area. I don't feel comfortable with a Baptist board at this point. In [the] end, I know I will feel comfortable in the will of God" *(June 10, 1986)*. My non-denominational home church and my studies on cultural issues on the field continued to challenge my perspective and who to serve with. In my mind, the agency would give much perspective on the approach to the task on hand. During that time, some Baptist boards would not take a sending church that was a Bible one. Although I liked the doctrine, I felt that I wanted to bring the Bible to the least-reached, not just my denomination.

Ironically, I have partnered mainly with Baptists in Central Asia and the Middle East throughout my many decades of service.

Things seemed to click that summer with me and WOL, so I wrote, "After this summer [1986], I feel a lot stronger about going with WOL as a missionary. I know I could do more, would feel more comfortable, could develop my gift of preaching,[49] and I would know the men I will be working with would be sound and disciplined. I've been praying a lot about it, and I know I will know by the end of next summer" [Muslim Outreach Training with Christar was planned.](Aug. 23, 1986).

Years later, when I told Dan I was engaged to a WOL appointee, he wrote back, "Don [Lough, Jr.] said that it would be great if you would come with WOL and help to begin the WOL to the Muslims. There is a Muslim in Argentina who was in the PLO [Palestine Liberation Organization] who would be interested in joining in this kind of endeavor as well" (Oct 14, 1994). He meant a *believer* from a Muslim background.

One morning in October, I woke to the sound of the phone. Where I lived, an international call rang differently than a local one. I knew something was up.

"Hello," I answered, fearing some problem or bad news.

"Hello, Jeff. Is this you?" Paul Bubar said.

I responded, "Yes... hello, Mr. Bubar. What a surprise to hear from you."

"I am so glad to connect with you, and I wanted to congratulate you on your engagement."

"Thanks so much." I was still trying to fathom why Paul Bubar was calling me.

He continued, "Well, you know we have known you a long time and know that you are called to minister with Muslims. We need people like you to be missionaries with WOL. We want to reach out to Muslims through our programs."

Though it was great to hear from Mr. Bubar, I was feeling a bit uneasy hearing all the words I'd learned to regard as taboo. In our country in the Middle East, we did not talk about missionaries or

Muslims in public or over the phone. The term "missionary" was often misunderstood as intent to overthrow the government — obviously not my goal.

He continued, "We would like you and Sharon to join us, helping us start a Muslim ministry. Since she was planning on going to Argentina, you both could go there and develop our Muslim work…"

When Sharon and I discussed Muslim ministry, I repeatedly mentioned spending 15 years in Central Asia to plant one church. In my research, I figured it would take at least that to see something start in an area with no church. It was a long-term commitment.

At that point, I was unsure what to say, but I always seemed to have some response regarding plans. "Well, I'm honored you thought of me. I don't feel I have enough experience working with Muslims yet, but maybe after 15 years of doing the work and starting a church or two, then I might be up for it maybe."

At that point, I thanked him and said we would pray about it, but I was still determined to head to a least-reached area to plant a church.

Over the years, I have considered the differences, and another worker who has been a part of both organizations summed it up like this: "Of course, WOL and Christar are quite different in ministry focus. Christar has a strong emphasis on church planting work, which I recognize as fundamentally significant. We made a switch because we recognized the need to place our energies in seeing churches planted and those multiplied."[50]

Dan and I debated the difference for years, and certainly both types of agencies see churches planted and multiplying. However, I sensed a calling to place my energies toward the church-planting model.[51]

Wedding - 1995

"Butler, you beat me." Those were the words I heard Dan say. "How so?" I asked.

"You will be getting married before I do," he said.

As we continued on the phone, I asked, "So when can you come and be my best man?"

"May is a good time because it comes after some spring outreaches and before summer. I could make a short visit to the States for your wedding," Dan said.

With that, the wedding was set for May 1995 in New York. My bride-to-be and I planned a simple wedding. She had only a maid of honor, Marlene, who had led her to the Lord. On my side, my best and only man was Dan. These two prayed a dedication at our wedding. We had a cake reception at our church and then a picnic reception at Sacandaga Bible Conference.

The music was a little more complex. We are not entirely sure of the details surrounding it, but we believe we asked Don Lough Jr. to play the piano for the entrance song, accompanied by a flutist, and Don Lough Sr. to play the trumpet for the exit song. The latter was unsure if he could make it, so his son, Don Lough, Jr., played the piano for the entrance and exit songs. Thinking back on this, we believe he sightread both pieces — flawlessly, actually. At least, that impression stays with us as his ability to do this well. We asked Don Sr. to play the trumpet at the wedding, but he was unable to commit to us for that weekend. Yet he still showed up for the wedding, for which we are thankful.

After the wedding ceremony receiving line, my new wife and I were rushed towards the gymnasium, where over 200 guests awaited our arrival. Before we could make this grand entry, though, the county clerk needed our signatures in the nearby office. Dan took the marriage certificate and quickly signed his name as a witness.

When I stepped up to sign it, there was Dan's signature in the space marked Groom. "Bubar, you are not marrying my wife! You just signed in my spot!" We all laughed it off, but the clerk had to rush to the town office for a new form and pick up another copy so Sharon could be officially married to me, not Bubar. When she returned, all of us—yes, everyone there—guided him to the proper place to sign as a witness.

Can you trust Bubar?

Now, Bubar was a prankster, and though I loved that he was by my side on my wedding day, I also feared what he might do to me after the ceremony.

Back at TTU, we had taken a class on the Song of Solomon. One day, the professor said, "Marriage is sacred, and the wedding day is holy for the couple. No one should *ever, ever* do a practical joke on this day. It is a sin and goes against the sacredness of that day."

"Bubar, did you hear that? It is a sin to play a practical joke at a wedding," I warned.

159

"Yeah, Butler, don't you think of doing that on my day," he responded.

The teacher continued, "Playing a practical joke on the wedding day is a great shame and disgrace."

"Did you get that, Bubar? It's a great shame and disgrace. Put that in your notes and remember," I said.

Dan learned pranking from his father, a master prankster who was paid back at his own wedding when one of his friends wrote "Help!" on the soles of his shoes. When Mr. and Mrs. Bubar knelt in prayer, many in the audience saw the words and started laughing.

Over the years, we would often remind each other of our professor's words, especially on May 19, 1995, the eve of my wedding. Dan was in my room that Friday night and my luggage was hidden in the car trunk at my mother's place. I said, "Remember, no one should ever play a practical joke at a wedding since it's a very solemn day." But I knew Dan would try to cook up something.

On Saturday morning, I arranged my Bubar-proof plan with another friend, Tom, whom I trusted for such a time. I had been his best man at his wedding, where no practical jokes ensued. We arranged to meet in a parking lot not far from the church to park my car so no one would have access to it during the wedding or reception. Then he drove me to the church in his car. I thought I had guarded against any potential embarrassment. The night before, I had placed Sharon's and my suitcases in the trunk so that from Friday night on, they would be protected in the back of the vehicle.

The wedding ceremony was solemn and respectful, and Dan even had to say a prayer of dedication. The cake reception was without incident.

We had a picnic reception at the lake, which allowed us to visit with our friends and family in a more informal setting. My sister approached me and said, "I have to talk to you."

"What's up?" I asked. She had a bag in her hand.

This is the story, as told by my sister, Janet:

The night before Jeff and Sharon's wedding, Dan, Jeff's best man, approached me and said, "Hey, I need your help."

Dan held up a set of keys, grinning. "I found the keys to Jeff's car."

"Oh boy," I said, feeling hesitant yet oddly excited about helping Dan prank my brother. "What do you need help with?" I asked.

160

"Well, I'm going to mess with Jeff's suitcase, but I don't want to open Sharon's suitcase accidentally," Dan whispered rather sheepishly. We were in the kitchen, and Jeff was upstairs, so there was really no need to whisper.

"Ok," I said, "Let's do it!"

So, we went outside and went to the trunk. Jeff had gone to bed quite a while before, but we were both a little nervous about being caught. Hopefully, he wouldn't look out the hallway window or hear us through the open windows upstairs!

Dan unlocked the trunk and lifted the back, and the light came on in the trunk. We looked at both suitcases. "Which one do you think is his?" he asked.

They both were the same medium-colored blue and similar in size.

"Well, let me open this one on the right first and check and see," I said.

"Okay, I'm going to turn around, just in case it's the wrong one..." Dan said as he turned.

Deep breath. This felt so very wrong. I would have been mortified if someone had looked into MY suitcase the day before my wedding and honeymoon!

I opened it up slowly, hoping it was Jeff's! I looked and saw something, and it didn't look like Jeff's clothes! "Nope, it's not this one!" I quickly shut it up.

Dan turned around and excitedly said, "This must be the other one!" He had that opened in a flash, and then I remembered that these were my brother's clothes, and I really didn't want to see what he packed for his honeymoon, either! So I turned, but I couldn't quite leave yet. Dan just made the whole thing quite daring and exciting!

"So what are you going to do to his stuff?" I whispered.

"Oh, nothing much..." he said, laughing.

"Dan?" I asked.

"Oh, I'm just taking all his underwear!"

The next day after the reception, when Jeff and Sharon were just about to leave, I remembered that I had that bag of his underwear in our car. My conscience was getting the best of me in the light of day, and I thought, "I can't let my brother go without his underwear! They'd have to find a store, and what if they weren't near a store? It would be a waste of money." So I grabbed the bag and handed it to Jeff.

"What's this?" Jeff asked, confused.

"It's your underwear."

So that was her story. I was thinking, "Oh, yeah, Bubar… a great sin to play a practical joke." My *solemn* sister was quite worried. Before she handed the bag to me, she confessed the whole caper to my new bride. At that moment, Glenn, Janet's husband and our photographer, happened to capture my wife's expression on camera. Her horrified expression has a spot in our wedding album, reminding us of Dan's hilariously "shameful" behavior.

Bubar explained later, "Hey, it was not my idea, and I did not physically take the items out of the suitcase; I only supplied the keys for the joint adventure." Since he wasn't alone, he was acquitted — in his mind. Glenn must have been involved with Bubar, but my sister did not mention her husband. Hmm.

I can recall my keys being in my coat pocket… downstairs—my mistake. Never trust a Bubar at a wedding!

Chapter Fourteen - Not Word of Life but WOL-like

In Central Asia, we collaborated with several families from New Zealand. Always looking for more produce options, I asked if they could bring me a kiwi seedling the next time they visited their country. They responded that a kiwi vine takes about seven years to produce fruit. Some good things require a great deal of time and care to yield their full potential.

Like the kiwi, our Central Asian calling was to prepare for and eventually bear fruit. Starting even one church required a long-term commitment, which, in turn, required constant care and spiritual nourishment.

When we were engaged, I mentioned the necessity of living in Central Asia for at least 15 years. She asked why that specific length of time. I sensed that God's plan to establish a Central Asian church would take about that long. Establishing a church requires living in a community long enough to learn its language and culture, helping them gather and organize in a way relevant to them, and then backing away.

I sometimes wondered what WOL would do in a country with no church, believers, or social agencies for promoting the gospel. After much prayer and surveying, along with language learning, we began to share the gospel with young people; they are the future of the church, the future students at Bible schools, and the future leaders who will proclaim the gospel. So, this is what I felt led to do, unknowingly applying Word of Life methods.

My call to church planting, for the most part, was a call to the least-reached. In Central Asia, that meant the following:

- In 1990, they estimated there was only one Central Asian believer in our country, and there were no churches in the local language.
- In 1998, the city we moved to — one of the country's largest — had no church, unlike some areas that had Russian or international churches.
- The nearest second-language church building was 1.5 hours away by car.
- Our team was initially the only Christian expats in the city.
- We needed some creative methods to influence the region.

For years, Dan and I debated: Church planting or WOL? Dan's rhetoric was that church planting was a buzzword. Mine was that it was a systematic method not used by WOL. Yet, when I needed creative methods, I returned to my background and experiences, namely, Word of Life.

Our main work was at social homes, where many needy children lived full-time, a remnant of the Soviet Union's system. Many were poor or single-parent children, with a few true orphans also included. This job provided the visas necessary to stay in the country.

Rallies in Central Asia

As foreigners, we were asked constantly by locals to teach English. However, we had been given two warnings regarding our work: teaching English sidetracks you from ministering in the local language, and you cannot plant a church through children. So, we regarded our social home job as the platform that kept us in the country and our church-planting efforts as anything else.

We tried lots of tactics. Jack Wyrtzen held rallies, and so could we. We would throw parties and share the gospel on special occasions such as Christmas and Resurrection Day, sometimes housewarming parties, sometimes when guests were visiting. We did not hold large public meetings but instead used public places like the university cafeteria or larger homes.

As we addressed this legitimate need in society, we also adopted Floyd McClung's statement: "It's God's work to bring people to Jesus—our work is to find the ones He's preparing and to work with them." Through these celebrations, we broadly spread the gospel seed, praying God would bring in those He had prepared.

Clubs in Central Asia

Nevertheless, our hearts were burdened for the children in the social homes. How could we reach them? When I visited Central Asia, I heard about the moral void the former Soviet Union had left. The country had lots of national propaganda but lacked basic human ethics.

So, on that short-term trip, fresh out of a Christian Education background at seminary, I suggested starting a Life Club that taught basic ethics using Scripture and local stories. These clubs were pre-evangelism-type clubs from a biblical worldview. We included both biblical and secular stories with ethical themes and helped them memorize certain Proverbs and local poems relating to a moral principle. The classes were not open evangelism but rather addressed a felt need. We aimed to enhance the lives of those we served and shared gospel truths as much as the circumstances allowed.

Camps in Central Asia

The Life Club met weekly during the school year, but what about the summer? The grounds of the social home seemed to be the best option for doing camp, and we proceeded to draw up a strangely familiar camp program.

Our first camp was at a social home, where the staff never liked what we were doing. During the school year, they enforced silence at mealtimes, so why would anyone play games and do challenges during that time? Afterward, the director said, "You ruined our place with your games during meals. Now they're noisy. No kid should be talking while they eat." We differed here.

Additionally, the living conditions in the camp were unhealthy and unsanitary. The water from the fields flowed through the school boarding area in the ditch and was as muddy as possible. This was where they washed their shoes, and this was the water they used for cooking. My wife, on her "millionth" trip to the outhouse one night, said she looked up at the big Dipper and deliriously began to imagine muddy water pouring out of it. At this camp, we all fell ill due to the contaminated water. Many children also became ill, but for them, it was a way of life, and many were visibly malnourished. We needed a new approach for future camps.

Praise the Lord. The following summer, we found our city's university camp, which was available from the end of May to the end of June. So, during the cooler months of the scorching summer, we spent four weeks of camps up in the mountains, where the water was fresh. We did this for four years, and in our final year, we had over 200 kids — all of whom were unsaved. Our camp program in this Muslim country continued the themes from the Life Club. We taught English and ethical Bible stories and played tons of games.

During the meals, we had challenges for the two teams. Our themes were friendship, leadership, family, and hope for the future. We incorporated backward days and international days, and eventually, I adopted an Island theme I heard about in the early

1980s — *What happens next? We don't know!* This relates to the theme of hope for the future and to trust the Lord in what happens. We pulled out all the stops, and one night, after they were all in bed, we woke them all up again to have a New Year's celebration. We hope these camps will be lifetime memories for those who came — they all knew we were Christians, and they heard many Bible stories. In a dominantly Muslim country, these activities were pre-evangelism and created a thirst to know God, which eventually happened for some of these kids.

Although the kids loved camp and looked forward to our weekly classes, some adults grew concerned about the outside influence. Eventually, we received complaints and needed to stop the camp activities. The local government intervened and established a protocol for my activities, stating that I could no longer work with children.

This led me to the next step.

Bible School in Central Asia

I changed my visa situation to work alongside a German mission that partnered with the country's evangelical churches. They had some local pastors, but they all used Russian instead of the national language in their ministry.

In God's timing and movement, their German director had been praying for years to see a Bible school in the local language. This opened up a door for our work, as I had desired to do exactly that—start a Bible school in the local language.

We agreed on ten sessions to cover Theology, Bible Survey, and practical ministry topics. When the 15 or so Central Asians gathered, we studied for five consecutive days, with classes held in the morning and afternoon. We had daily chapel and prayer together, praying for our country of residency. This was the program for each of the ten modules.

Although Dan and I had very different lives, each with distinct callings, I incorporated many of Word of Life's methods into my ministry. (So much so that later, when my son, Darius, ended up doing some WOL camp programs in Korea and the region, he said, "Now I know what you were doing in Central Asia—you were doing Word of Life.")

We even ended each week with a campfire and skits. I wanted them to change how they lived, become open to God's love, and live for the God who died for them, but the invitation had to differ.

Though we shared biblical truth and Gospel nuggets, the environment resisted a full invitation.

When the authorities eventually kicked us out of the country, they said we turned the city upside down. I was shocked one day when a 10-year-old boy came up to me on the street and started singing in the local Central Asian language, "This is the day that the Lord has made." I was glad to meet him but did not recognize him. I asked him if he had been at camp with us, and he said, "No." I realized the other kids were sharing songs and stories they had learned at camp.

Our call is a story bigger than ourselves since God himself has a bigger-picture plan. The US director of Christar, Steve Coffey, said that our ministry is "the story of salvation [that] God is sovereignly weaving throughout the nations and across time as He creates access for the gospel and draws people into His family." We were awed to be part of His story.

Chapter Fifteen - Dan Crosses the Finish Line

While attending the Bible Institute together in 1984, in our joint race that fall, I could only see Dan crossing the finish from a distance. In life, Dan ran the race persistently and thoroughly. He served right up to the moment of his death. At the time of his accident, which took place on May 1, 1996, he had just written what would be his last prayer letter. On May 10, after being transported to Munich, Germany, he was pronounced dead, having crossed the finish line. His funeral in Pottersville took place on May 20.

Camp at Tóalmás – Jan-Feb 1996

That winter, and I am not sure this was the normal routine, they had winter camp at a "castle lodge in the middle of nowhere in northern Hungary" (from his last Prayer Letter - dated May 10, 1996). This was most likely a form of outreach to a new area. He mentions that despite losing all power and heat on New Year's Eve, they had a fantastic camp with many decisions for Christ.

After this camp, Dan visited Ukraine, and Jorge Radziviluk led the WOL ministry. This expanded his focus and linked these two ministries. Dan often mentioned the importance of mutual sharing and collaboration at joint conferences. During the spring of 1996, the Ukrainian government continued to emerge from the USSR with new currency and eventually formed its new constitution in June of 1996. Before this point, Ukraine had become one of the first former Soviet regions to sign on to NATO's partners for peace (Feb. 1994). So with this openness, WOL ministries in Eastern Europe were a priority.

In Dan's letter, he described the stage of youth work during these initial years of WOL Hungary like this: "If one word could describe our club ministry this winter, it would be EVANGELISM! Week after week, we held evangelistic outreaches in various clubs using mini-concerts, banquets, slide shows, 'jalopy raids' and various sports. Many weekends, Word of Life staff were in two or three different clubs evangelizing, not only in the clubs evangelizing but also in the churches on Sunday!" (Prayer Letter - May 10, 1996).

He mentioned that the WOL clubs numbered 17 and had experienced significant spiritual growth, but the number of teens attending had decreased by 15%, as the initial novelty of the clubs had settled into a routine.[52] The call for discipleship is the same for all teenagers; few will step forth and truly live for God. Another notable point is that from 1995 to 1996, Hungary faced an economic challenge characterized by rising inflation and falling wages, which likely led some teenagers to start working to support their families.[53] An IMF report stated, "All policies that Hungary has already implemented—put heavy strains on real incomes and government finances."[54] Dan may have alluded to the difficulties of youth ministry and the economic situation when he said, "Our mid-winter conference was attended by all the clubs, and leaders left with a renewed dedication to 'stick by the stuff' in the ministry to which God has called them!" (Prayer Letter – May 10, 1996).

William Temple said Christians are "called to the hardest of all tasks: to fight without hatred, to resist without bitterness, and in the end, if God grant it so, to triumph without vindictiveness."[55] These days were filled with the need to endure for him and myself. Opposition takes many forms.

Dan, the Bible School Professor

Dan had a Bachelor of Arts in Bible, but the new Bible Institute at Tóalmás asked him to teach the History, Theology, and Tendencies in Missions. He said, "Teaching for a week here in the Bible Institute… gave me a new appreciation of the work done by our three resident professors. Ten hours in the classroom, a syllabus in English and Hungarian, quizzes and tests, and, on top of that, speaking in two languages reminded me of why the Lord called me to be an evangelist" (Prayer Letter - May 10, 1996). His Hungarian became quite fluent, so he translated and, with local help, likely wrote the Hungarian syllabus.

He planned to speak to the student body again in May, but this opportunity never came. However, he did mention another teaching opportunity that came his way, "Teaching at the Baptist Mission School in Budapest once a week with Eric Murphy has also given us the occasion to influence the future spiritual leaders of this country with a philosophy of youth ministry" (Prayer Letter - May 10, 1996).

His experience brought him into the classroom, and these teaching opportunities were a great honor. Yet he knew he was an evangelist and would do that instead.

Who is the Hero?

In a call to missions, we are not the hero of the story, but the one we follow—the Lord Jesus Christ. We do not know God's ways or thoughts, as they are beyond us. His dealings with men are above our comprehension. He allows plot twists and surprise endings. His purpose is for all nations to come before Him and worship Him; we get to be His channels for the message.

Since Dan lived in a castle, he thought now was the time to find a princess. His father wrote about that time: "He had fallen in love with a beautiful Hungarian woman, the daughter of one of our Board members, 'the young capitalist,' Zoltan Kavocs… Dan loved her and wanted to make her his wife — he just had to be patient for her love for him to develop more fully."[56]

When I got engaged, Dan's interest in knowing God's will in whom to marry started to consume his mind: "It would be great to sit down and chat with you for a while over how you knew that she was the one for you, etc." (Oct. 14, 1994). This conversation repeated itself the day before Sharon's and my wedding in 1995 and continued to be at the center of his mind during the final year of his life.

Then he wrote about his living situation, "I moved into a house in the village. I rent it for $150 a mo., without utilities. With utilities, it will run about the same as I was paying for my quarters in the castle. You'll have to come and see it. Three rooms, an entryway, a kitchen and bathroom, and a mutt dog" (underline original, Oct. 14, 1994). Most likely hoping to settle down, he'd found a place in town. This provided more space for him and most likely helped him to separate work from downtime. It also put him among the people.

The Lord never promised us that we would marry, but He did promise us an eternal home, which He has prepared for us and made a reality. Dan's days were marked on God's calendar.

Accident

God has sketched our days, and there is no such thing as an accident in God's plan. - Paul Bubar

We were in Saskatoon, Saskatchewan, when I heard that Dan was in an accident. The timing was approximately three days after the incident, as it took some time for the news to reach me. Hearing it, I was in total denial, thinking the incident was minor and that Dan would make it through. However, when I heard that Dan was in a coma, I was pretty distraught, and my emotions were raw with sorrow. Yet I was still hopeful he would pull through. Dan fought hard in whatever he faced. Now, he was fighting to live and to make it through this accident — these thoughts comforted me.

At the beginning of May, our church in Saskatoon had a communion service, and the reality of death hit me as I thought of the death of Christ. I wanted to partake in remembrance of the Lord, but his death, alongside Dan's possible death, overwhelmed me. I wept instead. *Do this in remembrance of me*" took on a new meaning as I remembered Dan living his life for others, just as Christ did. I thought of Christ's death and prayed Dan would pull through.

Later, I discovered that on May 1, 1996, near 11 p.m., an accident occurred on the highway outside Budapest while Dan was driving home from dropping off missionaries at the airport. As his father related, "Suddenly, out of the blackness of the night, without warning, came a heavily loaded tandem trailer that had broken free from the truck pulling it. There were no lights, nothing, only a loud crash. Dan did not see or hear anything." The brunt of the impact zeroed in on Dan. The female passenger grabbed the steering wheel and brought the car under control. Amazingly, "she was spared from even receiving as much as a scratch or bruise."

Paul Bubar also wrote appropriately, "Psalm 139:16 tells us that before we were born, God scheduled our days. Verse 17 tells us that God's thoughts are about us as the sand. In other words, God's thoughts about us are beyond counting. But those verses applied not only to two hurting parents but to our son as well. In other words, if God's thoughts about us are perpetual, that means that at the very moment that loaded trailer broke loose in the middle of the dark night and struck our son's auto, God was thinking about him too!"[57]

The news was initially sparse but became fuller with the Bubars' update letters. Our church, with its strong connection to Word of Life, informed me of any news they heard, as well as my mom, who received the newsletters. The damage to Dan's brain was unrecoverable despite care in Budapest first and then in Germany. Eventually, his heart stopped, and he entered into eternity. His mom summed this point up, saying, "The doctors assured us that, had he been traveling three miles per hour slower or three miles per hour faster, or if he had sat three inches lower like an average

Hungarian, he would have sustained the injuries and probably come through the difficulty. Oh, my dear friends, this was no accident—it was a divine appointment.[58]

Sharon's and my travels took us to the Minneapolis area to meet with our new team, who were heading to Central Asia. Together, we prayed and planned for the future of the church planting work there. At the same time, we all prayed for Dan's healing from this tragic accident. The hope of future ministry I previously wrote about was dampened by the inward sorrow I felt. On May 10, we heard that he had no brain waves and that he was declared dead. This news hit hard. *Why, Lord, did you take his life so suddenly?*

He was the third person I knew well that died way too young. Michele Wilson, my sister's best friend at the age of 16, Mark Kramm, who studied with me at TTU and DTS, had died a few months earlier of cancer at the age of 32 (Feb 12, 1996), and now Dan. All three desired to serve in an overseas situation, but Dan was the only one to die overseas. Was this some cruel irony that whoever desired to serve the Lord overseas would die young?

Bruce Hepner worked with Dan the last week of Dan's life. He said, "We toured the schools, churches, and cultural halls. During those first three days of ministry, some 94 young people came to Christ during that week….At one point, we had a fifteen-minute break, and I was dead tired, but Dan dragged me over to a girls' school and invited some of the girls to come to the meeting that night. Well, over 30 of them came to Christ that night… When we packed up and we were driving out of the driveway and two girls stopped us. They said, 'We heard that others made a decision, how can we do the same?" Well at that point, Dan turned off the car ignition and got out of the car and led the two girls to Christ."

Reflecting on Dan's Life

We drove to Schroon Lake to attend Dan's funeral at Mountainside Bible Chapel on our first wedding anniversary. Irony ruled the moment. Exactly a year earlier, Dan stood beside me as my best man. He prayed the prayer of dedication for our marriage, even praying for our future children, including our two-month-old Darius, who lay in his baby carrier on the day of Dan's funeral.

In 1995, in correspondence before the wedding, Dan seemed to prophesy with these words, "Yes, Butler, I'll be in your ~~funeral~~ wedding in May." As a jokester, he wrote it that way intentionally.

Now, ironically, I was at his funeral one year later as one of six pallbearers whose hands carried his coffin.

Pastor Roger Ellison's opening words ring true: "We're here to rehearse what we believe about the reality of eternity."

Comments at the Funeral:

"God took Dan earlier than we expected and earlier than we planned for." – Paul Bubar

"He never was happier in his life than at the time that his life ended. He was doing what he always dreamed of doing. He was ecstatically happy in the ministry." – Paul Bubar

"A week ago, we had a memorial service in Hungary for Dan… five young people accepted the Lord." – Eric Murphy

"Many people are saying to me, 'I'm sorry you lost your friend.' — I did not lose anyone; I know exactly where they are. They only changed their address. 'Absent from the body, present with the Lord.' " – Harry Bollback

"Paul and Shirley, Danny was yours but also Danny was ours. Danny was, for this pastor, what makes all the efforts and difficulties more than worthwhile. And he came through all our programs, Sunday school, our academy, our youth program. He was active and consistent both as a teenager and a young man. Also, we heard of his ample effectiveness as a missionary." – Pastor Roger Ellison

"The Word of God is true, and God is a gracious and merciful God, who took our son before we wanted him to, as any parent ever wants God to take a son. Our faith is not worthless but is real." – Paul Bubar

"Dan Bubar had biblical hope. It was certain. It was the anchor of his soul, the certainty of hope." – Joe Jordan

"He loved this country very much. Just ten days before his accident, he had a meeting in our church, and four people made a decision for Christ. These four never came to church before. And this was his whole life, to save people." – Pastor Kovac

"I had the privilege to serve the last time with Dan Bubar on Tuesday, just two days before his accident. I served with Dan in a state school. There were more than 80 non-believing students and five teachers. They were really touched by the words of Dan… he preached the gospel clearly on that Tuesday." – Pastor Tibor

"And I wondered over the past few days: Who is going to dare to pick up where Dan left off? Who's going to have the same courage, and the same commitment, and the same compassion which Dan

175

showed us with his life? Who will dare to be a Daniel…Bubar?" Don Lough, Jr.

At Daniel Bubar's celebration of life, although I was not on the list of speakers, his dad saw me and requested that I say something during the service. I shared some of the fun we had together and how I labeled him "a bundle of stress poured out on people."

Then I recalled that precisely to the day, the year before, he stood at my side as my best and only man at my wedding. The night before my wedding, he stayed with me at my mom's house and said to me, "Butler, you beat me! You beat me in getting married." With those thoughts in my mind, my response to him at the end of his life was, "Bubar, you beat me; you beat me to Heaven!"

Dan's Heart

His father shared a story about Dan that I did not know until 25 years after Dan's death. Michael Kovacs, whom Paul met on a rerouted flight he happened to be on, often "loaned his influence" in government circles to benefit WOL Hungary.

Michael Kovacs had special dinners at his own home to which he invited politicians, Olympic athletes, actors, and other influential Hungarians. Along with these individuals, he invited Dan. When the conversation took off, Michael would direct a question at Dan: "Now, Dan, you are an American, but you are here. Do you have a girlfriend?" Dan would say, "No." Then he asked, "Then why are you in Hungary? What brought you here?" Dan then shared why he was in Hungary and presented the gospel. At times, Michael would walk out and let Dan continue. No one dared change the subject since the host had started the conversation. Dan, at these meals, had the chance to share the gospel with many influential Hungarians. Proverbs 22:29 says, "Do you see a man skillful in his work? He will stand before kings; he will not stand before obscure men."

Missionary Robin Brooks said, "Dan liked to have fun, yet he had a very serious side. He really cared deeply for the salvation of lost souls and that believers grow in their walk with God. He radiated the love of Christ to others."

In an interview with Paul Bubar, the interviewer said, "Describe some of the people who played an important role in the history of WOL Hungary." He answered, "Dan Bubar, great son, focused on doing the will of God. Loved the Hungarian people. He had a personality change as he became more Hungarian than he was American. And no regrets."

Perspective

Dan's life was dedicated to serving, and he did it well. He was an ordinary young person with typical personal quirks, yet he came at the right time to be used by God in a way that the Lord wanted him. I remember Dan's life verse, which he placed on his prayer card: "Faithful is He who calleth you, who also will do it" (First Thessalonians 5:23).

For an eternal God, His "now" encompasses the past, present, and future. He sees the full scope of history, encompassing what was, what is, and what will eventually be for us. Bubar was a constant companion in my past and remains in my memory. His smile, friendship, faith, his stress poured out, and his humor and stamina to serve still urge me on. Reflecting on our times together over the years, the stories have illuminated my memories and become folklore with my kids. I know those moments matter to me; his life made a difference for God and for me.

While in seminary, I recall a speaker who had studied at Oxford and conducted scientific research before deciding to enter the ministry. A colleague was surprised that he would give up a potentially successful career to serve God. In disbelief, he lamented, "It seems like a waste," to which the speaker replied, "Serving the Lord is never a waste."

From the perspective of those who seek only comfort and pleasure in this world, spiritual work is considered a waste. Sadly, their pursuits will come to an end with them. But Dan did not waste his life; instead, he spent it on eternal treasure. The gospel-spark he started in the WOL program in Hungary will glow for generations. He loved Hungary and the Hungarians.

God's heart for His crown of creation is evident from the start. In the Garden of Eden, even after Adam and Eve sinned, the Lord God was present, calling out to them and providing for them. Throughout history, His heart has been for people to come to know Him and represent Him.

At Paul Bubar's Celebration of Life in April 2021, Dan's mom, Shirley, spoke and challenged more than reminisced. She said, *Live for eternity!* The life we remembered that day epitomized that directive. Both Paul and Dan lived for eternity. I thought, *What a* great summary. *Live for eternity!* Through all the memories, challenges, and joys we shared, this refrain shaped our thinking: our life is not our own, but the Lord's, and we live for eternity.

For those who pass away in the Lord, they are more alive today than ever before. Shirley Bubar said at Paul's funeral, "The world looks at the internal and external but not the eternal. The Christian life is lived by faith from an eternal perspective."

On this occasion, she quoted twice from the C.T. Studd poem that the WOL Island placed on a sign: "Only one life, 'twill soon be past; only what's done for Christ will last," a philosophy of ministry that encompasses what a dedicated life to Christ is all about. What will last from the past? To live for Christ is to deny self, take up the cross, and follow him.

Dan's grave located in Pottersville, NY - his parents lived next to this cemetery.

The following is a fitting example of how God used the story of Dan in the lives of others:

One of the last people to see Dan alive was the man Dan and his girlfriend dropped off at the airport. Dan's sudden death spoke into this man's life, and he said, "You will never know how that impacted my life, truly. I had never known anyone close to me who had died before then, and it was the first time I was confronted with the fragility of life! When I received the word that he had died within only a few minutes after leaving me, I was broken and was forced to grapple with my own mortality. It was after that I told the Lord He could have my life, and I would serve Him."[59] WOW!

The last stanza of the poem brings the finality of life to a close:

Only one life, yes only one,
Now let me say, "Thy will be done;"
And when at last I'll hear the call,
I know I'll say "'twas worth it all;"
Only one life, 'twill soon be past,
Only what's done for Christ will last.
(C.T. Studd)

178

If you enjoyed this book, please leave a review or promote the book by posting your thoughts on social media. My goal is not to sell more books but to promote a resource I think will significantly help many people. Thanks and blessings!

To make personal comments, testimonies, and insights on this writing, please contact me on Facebook or Linkedin – Nakhati Jon.

For those interested in Word of Life, please see https://www.wol.org/ or ministry to the least-reached see https://www.christar.org/

Appendix

Letters of Remembrance

During the few days before Dan's death, his parents sent out a few letters for information and prayer. They are listed below.

To: Dan Bubar Friends and Prayer Warriors
From: Paul & Shirley Bubar,
Date: May 3, 1996
RE: Dan's Condition Update
Dear Friends

Shirley and I arrived in Budapest on Thursday morning, May 3. We were met at the airport by Eric Murphy and Laci Kadar. We went immediately to the Saint Janos Hospital Intensive Care Unit to see our Daniel. He was struck by an out of control Coca Cola truck trailer. He was in the right lane of a four-lane highway with no median barrier. The trailer was in a skid and came out of the night with no warning. The point of impact was in Dan's door. He had only time to turn his head. His girlfriend, Kinga Kovacs, was uninjured and grabbed the wheel, steering the car and keeping it from crashing again. Dan took a direct hit in the head by the careening trailer. He has massive head trauma to the brain. Rescue workers had to cut him from the auto.

He is stabilizing — kidney function, blood pressure, heartbeat, etc. He cannot breathe on his own and is on a life-support ventilator. The local doctors are not optimistic because of the swelling of the brain. American neurologist specialists, however, have encouraged us by saying what is happening is normal under the circumstances.

He must remain on the ventilator for a week or more until the swelling of the brain subsides. We are optimistic. Little did I know a week ago when I spoke in our Bible Institute chapel on "The Ministry of Tears" that Shirley and I would be given that ministry so quickly.

Pray for Dan. Pray that God will shrink the swelling of his brain. If that happens, he has a chance of returning to normalcy.

In a wonderful Missions Conference at the Calvary Baptist Church in Oshawa, Ontario, Canada, the night of Dan's accident, I had preached on I John 5:14-15. The idea is praying in the will of God. Dan is in the will of God here. He is successfully doing the will of God. He was wonderfully happy in his ministry.

John said if we pray in the will of God, we will have the petitions we ask of him. Will you "spread the word" to raise up an army of prayer warriors? If God should decide to take Dan home, we are prepared to accept that, but we truly believe God will spare him. Will you believe and pray with supplication and thanksgiving with us? God is sovereign. He truly is. He makes no mistakes. We need your prayers now!

We will keep you posted. The Word of Life Hungary fax #'s are: 011-36-1-251-4575 (Budapest office); #011-36-29-426-003 (Tóalmás Castle)

We are, as Jack used to say, "living on the victory side!"

Special Fax to Family, Friends and Supporters of Dan Bubar
Munich, Germany, May 10, 1996

"I have fought the good fight, I have finished the race, I have kept the faith. Finally, there is laid up for me the crown of righteousness, which the Lord, the righteous Judge, will give on that day, and not to me only, but also to all who loved His appearing" (II Timothy 4:7-8).

Yesterday, we flew Daniel by Air Ambulance from Budapest to Munich to be under the observation of the finest doctors in Europe. After many tests, it was conclusively determined that our wonderful son, Daniel Ray Bubar, went into the presence of his Lord whom he loved so much at 1:00 p.m. EST (7:00 p.m. Munich time). His race is finished. He is finally Home.

It is very clear to us that it was Dan's time to go Home. Everything... everything about this incident was so specific... a crowded highway... a careening heavily loaded trailer out of the night... hitting Dan only... all the efforts to spare Dan's life, including an emergency Air Ambulance to the most credible Medical Center in Europe... the top neurosurgeons — all to hold on to Dan. We wanted to know before the Lord that we had done all we could for Daniel. But it was Dan's time to end his great ministry here on earth and enter into the presence of his Lord (Psalm 139:16). Dan was deliriously happy in his ministry. Bringing young people to his Savior was his delight, his food, his sleep, his dream time, his very life.

Shirley and I, with Don Johnson, return to Hungary tomorrow for a Memorial Service at Tóalmás Castle on Tuesday night at 6:00 p.m. We will bring Dan's body home before week's end for burial at Schroon Lake. At this writing, a Memorial Service is being planned for Monday, May 20, at 1:00 p.m. at Dan's home church, the Mountainside Bible Chapel in Schroon Lake, New York.

We ask that you not send flowers, but if God should lead, you may contribute to the Dan Bubar Memorial Fund, which will be used to further the ministry of Bible Clubs to the Hungarian youth.

We want all to know that God has been glorified through Dan's life and Homegoing. We, as parents, have no regrets. Only those who have sent a son or daughter on ahead of them understand the hurt, but our God truly is sufficient in every situation (II Corinthians 3:5).

Pray for Eric Murphy and the Hungarian ministry that this strategic ministry will have someone to fill Dan's leadership role. Eric will need much wisdom and help.

We truly are on the victory side,
Paul & Shirley Bubar

Memorial to Dan from David Bubar

On May 1st, 1996 my younger brother Daniel Ray Bubar was one moment with the woman he loved and the next with the Lord he loved. This is a time of strong emotion for me; I am both grieved and content. I am grieved because it may be many years before I will get to see him again. Content because I know I will see him again someday when I too pass into eternity. I know this to be true for it was the apostle Paul who wrote that "If there is no resurrection from the dead, then not even Christ has been raised. And if Christ has not been raised, our preaching is useless and so is your faith. More than that, we are then found to be false witnesses about God, for we have testified about God that he raised Christ from the dead. But he did not raise him if in fact the dead are not raised. For if the dead are not raised, then Christ has not been raised either. And if Christ has not been raised, your faith is futile; you are still in your sins. Then those who have fallen asleep in Christ are lost. If only for this life we have hope in Christ, we are to be pitied more than all men" – 1st Corinthians chapter 15 verses 13-19, NIV. Please read the entire passage at your own leisure.

I loved my brother, we were only 2 years apart and I will miss him terribly, I already do. But I know that my brother Dan lived his life according to the principles and dictates found in the Bible. He knew what was right and he did it no questions asked. How did he know? He studied his Bible and prayed. He prayed for wisdom and direction, and you know what? God gave it to him. When God took my brother home to be with him, he did it in a very precise manner. We believe, by looking at the wreckage, that Dan went to be with the Lord the moment of impact. He turned his head to look at his girlfriend Kinga, so he did not see the trailer coming. Kinga, sitting next to Dan didn't get a scratch on her. God chose to spare her life; I suppose for further ministry.

So long Dan, I love you. David Bubar

Letter from Sarah Bubar

Dear Dan,   May 12, 1996

It seems silly to write a letter I know will never be sent. But I just wanted to express to you what you've done for me. It's partly because of you that I am who I am.

I remember growing up as a child you wanted me to be a boy so you could have your even Basketball team… 2 on 2.

I remember, too, teasing I would get from you about being afraid of the dark. I was so afraid that the blackness would swallow me up like the monster in the closet did to my Barbie's minivan. You would calm me down with no sympathy whatsoever, reminding me that "I was such a baby"… imagine that at 6.

I remember as a young teenager, barely in the eighth grade, being **made** to start a quiz team at church. You supported me though, lying to me when you assured me that this was the "absolute funnest part of Teens Involved." You know that I never would have been on the Quiz team had you not been so enthusiastic about it. If you hadn't been there quizzing me on all 30 verses in the Word of Life Scripture Memory verse pack, I would have never stuck with it. And we went to Nationals every year… even won a couple times, too! I did it just for you.

You pushed me all the time to be the best I could be (without going into the army). You were my own personal drill sergeant (how lucky for me!). But I want to thank you.

Because of you, I am not afraid of the dark. In fact, the room has to be absolutely black for me to get any kind of sleep. (I even have to turn off those little candles Mom has in all the windows — those dumb things light up the entire room).

Because of you, I love to run. I'm no marathon runner and I'll probably never bring home a turkey from a race I win. But you gave me a love for running.

Because of you, I got an A on my verses while at the Bible Institute. My friends would all be racking their brains trying to remember these verses for five hours, while I had them memorized since eighth grade.. still do.

But I think, Dan, the greatest thing you've given me is my love for missions. It's because of you that at twelve years old I told God I'd go wherever, just like my big brother Dan. It's seeing your eyes light up when you see a young person responding to a message that has given me this desire. It's watching your perseverance and determination in learning the Hungarian language that has spurred me to that end. And it is hearing your testimony and reading of your love for the ministry that has cultivated that love in me. I don't know if Mom or Dad has told you, but I changed my major from Bible to Missions. And it's <u>because of you</u>.

Dan, there's one more thing that you've given to me. You gave it to me the day you left us. It was a longing for heaven. Before, I always loved life. I wanted to live till I was 100. I really truly wanted the Lord to tarry so I could live a long, meaningful life, filled with great things done for Christ. I wanted to live the kind of life Sophie Muller did. Live one patterned after our dear "Uncle" Jack. To be able to live life to its fullest capability. Now, I have a different point of view. Because of you, Dan, "For me to live is Christ" …. But to die… that would be so much gain!

Till we meet again… I love you
Your sister, Sarah

My Vigil – Jonathan Bubar

How do I begin to tell
The feeling in my heart, dear Lord?
For they flow deeper than the deepest well,
And time would not afford.

My brother's life is in the balance,
And teeters to and fro.
It all happened in sudden instance,
And so soon he could go.

My heart aches for I love him true,
But the aching is for me.

For if he goes to be with you,
He would be totally free.

He is my teacher and dearest friend,
Whose love was tough, yet tender.
He served You till the very end,
And all, to You, he'd render.

A testimony true and bright,
Of a man who did things Your way.
He did what he did because it was right.
And yet, now, here he lays.

I must confess, in honesty,
Lord, this does not make sense.
But then, with wisdom heavenly,
You truly know what's best.

I guess that I must not need
His words as I feel I do.
Maybe I need to really heed
The things he already told me to.

Things like, "Jon, listen to Dad.
He's wise and always right."
"Jon, don't let yourself get sad.
Get up and fight the good fight."

"And don't let turkeys get you down,
You're an eagle and meant to fly.
A turkey walks along the ground,
But an eagle, in the sky."

"Listen to instruction, Jon,
And always take advice."
"Don't listen to the foolish one,
But make friends with the wise."

"Lastly, Jon, don't be afraid
Of anything or anybody.
For that is a trap that Satan laid,

185

To turn you from stone to putty."

So if you decide his time is done,
And this his final day,
In my heart his <u>LIFE</u> still rings on,
Of one who did things Your way.

Jonathan Bubar – May 2, 1996

General Letter from Paul & Shirley – May 28, 1996

Please allow Shirley and me to address you through this general letter. We are overwhelmed and deeply humbled by the kind words and love expressed by literally hundreds of people like you who have followed us in prayer over the mountain tops and through the valleys. What a great God we serve! What a great family we have within the body of Christ.

Little did I know when I preached in our Bible Institute Chapel on the subject of *The Ministry of Tears*, on April 24, that exactly one week later Shirley and I would be given a crash course on the subject and be called upon to practice what I preach.

Wednesday night (5:00 p.m. EST) our missionary son, Daniel, in Budapest, would be in a horrible collision, suffering great head trauma, that would result in his being called to Heaven. His Hungarian sweetheart, Kinga Kovacs, would be spared without an injury. Thank you, Lord!

I left the meetings in Ontario, Canada. Shirley met me at JFK International Airport and we immediately flew to Budapest. My attorney friend, Don Johnson, immediately left his conference in Mexico City and met us at the ICU Ward in a Budapest hospital. Though we didn't know it until Dan had stabilized enough to fly by Air Ambulance to University Medical Center in Munich, Daniel's race was over here on earth. His body shut down in Germany on May 10.

Shirl told me, "I didn't know that at times like this, you literally ache on the inside." I stood by Dan's bedside and told the Lord I would gladly exchange places with him, were it possible to do so. But that was not in God's marvelous plan.

A Memorial Service was held at Word of Life Castle in Hungary attended by up to 500 friends, pastors and youth, some of whom he had led to Christ. A second Memorial Service was held here at Schroon Lake attended by another 500 family and friends. What a victorious service it was, being attended by many local unsaved people. Dan's body rests in the local cemetery barely 300 ft. from our home.

Our God was not asleep the night of Dan's accident. We believe Dan had a divine appointment (Psalm 139:15-16) and Shirley and I are completely at peace knowing that, in a very brief time, we will see our Dan again. He finished his race well.

A friend shared Isaiah 57:1-2 with us. These verses tell us that good men perish, godly men die before their time, and no one seems to wonder why or care. No one seems to realize that God is taking them away from evil days ahead. For the godly who die shall rest in peace. Dan is with his Lord, his grandparents, Uncle Jack Wyrtzen and many others. He is ecstatically happy, and we are totally at peace in this matter.

Thank you, thank you, thank you for your phone calls, cards, faxes and letters. Thank you for your gifts to the Dan Bubar Memorial Fund that will go to help fund Dan's Hungarian replacement. You have been such an encouragement to Shirley and me.

Enclosed [above] are copies of a poem, letter and eulogy by Dan's two brothers and his sister. You may enjoy them. Video and audio tapes were made of the Schroon Lake Victory Service should you request one.

Until the whole world knows about Christ,

Paul & Shirley Bubar
I Thess. 4:13-18

Bibliography

Interviews and Letters
- Audio memories from Jeff Street, 2021.
- E-mail Letters from Glenn Slothower, Don Lough, Jr., Charles F. Scheide, Howie Williams and Janet Sebast.
- Interviews with Jonathan Bubar and Sarah (Bubar) Dever, and Glenn Slothower.
- My journals from 1981 to 1996.
- Personal letters from Dan Bubar.
- Prayer letters of Dan Bubar.
- Greg Parson - Personal correspondence dated May 28, 2021.
- Audio memories from Jeff Street, 2021.

Online References
- *Remembering 20 Years, Harry Bollback,* https://www.youtube.com/watch?v=QbmGMgLRr9w.
- *Remembering 20 Years, Paul Bubar*, Word of Life Hungary interview, Part 1-4, YouTube.
- *The Life of Paul Bubar*, First Baptist of Warrensburg, Facebook video. May 18, 2020, accessed April 18, 2021.
- Sarah Bubar blog: https://unlockingfemininity.wordpress.com/2011/11/10/redeeming-pain/

Books
1. Bubar, Paul. *Not by Chance*. Delmar, NY : First Century Pub. 2004.
2. *Perspectives Instructors Guide* "Guidelines: World Christian Discipleship," Instructor Lesson 15, pdf.
3. Sanders, J. Oswald. *Spiritual Leadership* Chicago: Moody Press, 1989.

<hr>

[1] Lyrics by Charlotte Elliott and Music by William Batchelder Bradbury.

[2] 1943-2023, besides counseling, he ministered and interpreted for the deaf for over 40 years.

[3] Romans 3:10, 23; Romans 5:8; 6:23 and 10:9-10.

[4] "My teaching responsibilities with Word of Life recently came to a conclusion after 41 years (29 years as a guest lecturer and 12 full-time)." (email from Charles F. Scheide, Oct 24, 2018).

[5] The Covid pandemic shut it down in 2020 and they sold the property in 2021. https://www.adirondackexplorer.org/stories/lodge-at-word-of-life-in-schroon-lake-set-to-be-sold accessed Nov. 1, 2021.

[6] Summer Training Corps. The former name for summer staff.

[7] Teen Boys from various jobs stayed in what was called "Lodge B." Lodge B was located down the road from the Inn, where the guests stayed, and Lodge A was where youth leaders stayed while their teens were on the Island. The "A" could be an awesome place to stay, while "B" was definitely a B-rated place with multiple limitations.

The ample distance from the main adult Inn area was probably best, considering the chaos that 14 to 18-year-old boys can create. Our minds were unfettered by the chains of responsibility or thoughts about the outcomes of our actions. We had fun and did some silly things, and anyone who hears about these things later in life would ask, "What were they thinking?" But we weren't thinking; this was the beauty.

Our dorm was a jumbled mess of opportunities for mischief. It was old and frail, practically falling apart. It was the type of place you could complain about all day, but instead, we saw it as a playground. It was torn down in the middle of the following summer, and I'm sure our hectic adventures that summer contributed to that decision.

The Lodge was two stories tall, with cracks and holes between the floors. As the summer progressed, the male staff got more creative with utilizing the building's shortcomings. One of their best uses was for water fights and as a means of revenge.

We realized a closet on the second floor was filled with random holes and openings to the lower floor. A bunch of us guys worked on emptying the closet, and we listened to the lower floor as they ruminated on how to attack us next. The hole led straight to their dorm room, so it was the perfect opportunity to hit them with a sneak attack before they could attack us. One of the guys grabbed a hose (who knows where he got that from), and we stuck it through the floor and hosed the guys below. We were not concerned about water damage at that age.

[8] Camper-in-training (CIT) program began by at least 1964 and involved many key leaders in their early years, like Wayne & Ruthie Lewis and David Cox. It was usually a four-week program of intense discipleship in the wilderness. The daily program consisted of exercises that included running up and down Cardiac Hill. The campers attended morning Bible Hours and had a weekly quiz, verses to memorize, and daily Quiet Time. The Mt. Giant trip was an overnight trip, and the Mt. Marcy trip was a four-day trip with two overnights. Sometimes, counselors from Moody helped with the program. The first week of camp was typical. On the first Saturday, the group would climb Mount Pharoah (2,546 feet) or Mount Giant, then Mount Marcy (5,343 feet) the following Saturday, followed by a 40-mile canoe trip through Raquette Lake, Long Lake, and on to Tupper Lake during the last week. This program, known initially as Adirondack Wilderness Adventure, was shortened to three weeks in 1992. They learned fire safety, knot tying, and basic first aid on the wilderness trips.

[9] Paul Ralph Dilger (1942-2015). He worked a few years at WOL as a chef in the 1980s, most likely from 1982 to at least 1986. Obituary, https://www.tributearchive.com/obituaries/2560490/Paul-Ralph-Dilger

[10] Ebba Nilson Swanson, 1919-1997.

[11] Learning How to Bake

I enjoyed making chocolate cakes or cookies at home every week, so I was well-accustomed to measuring. Yet I was surprised when I entered the bakery to discover that measuring by weight, not volume, was the standard practice. I no longer needed cups and teaspoons but a scale. Some recipes called for 10 to 20 pounds of flour, so we had to fill the industrial metal scale container two to three times. Measuring the recipe with cups would have taken forever.

In the bakery world, 3-6 lbs of flour meant 3 pounds and 6 ounces.

This bakery was state of the art in the 1980s. It was part of the renovations that took place in 1970 when Doc Jensen[11] wanted to upgrade the entire kitchen, which had been in place since 1953, from its Brown Swan Club days. He was WOL's first food director, and he had a great bakery background. So, when he set up the Inn bakery, the equipment was sufficient for large-scale production. The upgrade fostered a positive and professional atmosphere, and Dan and I were among its beneficiaries.

I learned to use the antique Penn Cast Iron Bakery Scale to measure ingredients. First, I weighed the oval-shaped holder (tin scale scoop) and recorded the weight, adding it to the recipe's requirements.

For example, if the recipe called for 3-8 ounces of flour, I placed a two-pound weight on one end and adjusted the hanging weight to 24 ounces. Then, I added flour to the holder until the scale was balanced. If it tipped, I would add or remove small portions of flour until it was perfectly balanced and the arrow pointed to zero.

For liquids, the gallon container was key. I soon learned that one quart of water weighs about 2 pounds. Yet, not all liquids are equal in density, so items like oil, butter, and milk vary, and we needed to measure them differently according to the expected weight.

[12] Donald Burton Powell (1927-2019). The Food Director from 1982 to 1983 (?) at Word of Life.

[13] They met near my church at the Bible Memory Association Camp in Perth, NY, which is how their story connected to me. I was trying to get Dan off my back by giving him less information, increasing his curiosity.

[14] Story told by Carol Lough's perspective.

[15] Michele Lee Wilson 1965-1983, buried in Scotia, NY.
https://www.findagrave.com/memorial/20703624/michele_lee-wilson/flower

[16] Personal correspondence with Howie Williams, email dated Aug. 17, 2021.

[17] Details are available at:
https://www.independent.co.uk/news/obituaries/obituary-pastor-georgi-vins-1139170.html accessed Jan. 11, 2021. 1928-1998.

[18] I did try this method later with my wife-to-be. Interestingly, Georgi Vins' father, Peter Vins, was the son of Mennonite Brethren leader Jacob J. Wiens, who was born in Borden, Saskatchewan. My wife was also born in Borden.

[19] I also went forward at my home church's mission conference near that time.

[20] Don Lough, Jr. worked in the Garden Café in the summer of 1983, the first time they ran the Café as the main lunch option. Previously, the main dining room offered three meals daily; however, a new format was introduced in 1983. There was no lunch available at the Inn Clubhouse, but the café provided a place to grab a light lunch. It was quite a task to organize meals from the small space in the Garden Café, as most guests then habitually enjoyed lunch at the Inn; therefore, most guests had lunch there that summer. On a few occasions, Glenn Slothower asked me to come and help. I only recall the stress of attempting to produce quick meals and assorted desserts in that small prep area of the Café. Serving lunch along with ice cream orders proved challenging in such a small space. When finished, I was glad to return to the peaceful bakery in my own corner of the kitchen. Oh, I am too nostalgic for the Inn!

[21] Personal letter from Dan, Feb. 22, 1983.

[22] Vance Havner spoke during the summers of 1981, 1983 and 1985 based on Jeremy Biesecker, who documents some WOL history. He wrote Word of Life Camps, which appears to be out of print at present.
magic@illusionswithjeremy.com

[23] A version of this message is on YouTube: Called "Don't miss your miracle." https://www.youtube.com/watch?v=sjsXzvGLEXw accessed July 5, 2021.

[24] Proverbs 10:4. Since Dan memorized from the KJV, he quoted from this version.

[25] Most likely called the Gallop like in his letter but the embellished story seemed to use the Turkey Trot name. The Turkey Trot was in November but the Gallop in May.

[26] Both of these men have served decades in South America with WOL.

[27] © Copyright by Harry Bollback. Used by permission on July 19, 2021.

[28] Proverbs 16:9

[29] This promotion started in 1987.

[30] 1944-2024

[31] Missions' notes from Mickey Johnson, TTU, 1987. Passed in 2017, no birth year given. http://www.hamiltonfuneraloptions.com/obituary/4555888 accessed May 10, 2021.

[32] Near this time, Paul Bubar became head of Overseas Ministries and appointed missionaries. So, this was a relevant discussion he encountered.

[33] Sept. 22, 1988, at the Brainerd Mall in Chattanooga, TN.

[34] https://www.linkedin.com/posts/carlosahidalgo_feedback-growth-relationships-activity-7164257041744662528-ZNCM

[35] By the way Pat Robertson's wife Dede was saved on their honeymoon at Word of Life Inn.

[36] The school boasts that both Ted Turner, his son (IV), and a grandson graduated from there. In 1994, a few years later, Ted Turner endowed the school with $25 million.

[37] Oct 27, 1985, personal journal.

[38] April 22, 1989

[39] https://wordoflife.edu/paul-bubar-on-serving-jesus-christ-its-more-than-i-ever-dreamed/

[40] Paul Bubar. *Not by Chance*, 178.

[41] Ibid., 177.

[42] Chris Miller taught at WOLBI and, in the fall of 1991, became a professor of Biblical Studies at Cedarville in Ohio.

[43] The founding Director of WOLBI in Hungary. He served with WOL for 21 years.

[44] https://simplychurch.com/2012/07/20/the-amazing-story-of-sophie-muller/ She came to Christ on the streets where Jack Wyrtzen was preaching.

[45] These dates most likely include the travel days; later, he states that the event took place from April 1-3, 1994.

[46] Remembering 20 Years, Paul Bubar, Part 3, 2010. In an interview with Paul Bubar in 2010, he said that WOL Hungary is becoming a center of WOL activities throughout Europe. https://www.youtube.com/watch?v=8EIIxtdHDrk accessed April 17, 2021.

[47] May 20, 1996, at Dan's "Celebration of Life."

[48] Yes, but I later wrote a letter asking for his blessing and met him the day before the wedding — He was thrilled that his daughter was getting married.

[49] That summer, Ed Hart who oversaw a weekly Prison ministry, signed me up for a month of preaching.

[50] Personal correspondence with Howie Williams, email, Aug. 19, 2021.

[51] Since then, I have met some in WOL who have ministered effectively among Muslims.

[52] At Dan's funeral Harry Bollback said 18 clubs were started, and by the fall, hoped for 30 to be in place. May 20, 1996.

[53] https://www.elibrary.imf.org/view/IMF071/04653-9781557756992/04653-9781557756992/ch04.xml?language=en accessed March 29, 2021.

[54] IMG eLibrary, *4 Inflation in Hungary* 1990-97. Accessed March 29, 2021.

[55] Warren W. Wiersbe, *The Bible Exposition Commentary*, vol. 1 (Wheaton, IL: Victor Books, 1996), 427.

[56] Paul Bubar, *Not by Chance*, 202.

[57] *Ibid.*, 204.

[58] Shirley Bubar at the "Celebration of Daniel Bubar," at Mountainside Bible Chapel, May 20, 1996.

[59] https://unlockingfemininity.wordpress.com/2011/11/10/redeeming-pain/ accessed July 19, 2021.

www.ingramcontent.com/pod-product-compliance
Lightning Source LLC
Chambersburg PA
CBHW072001040426
42447CB00009B/1432